MW00800489

Dedicated
with kind permission
to H.R.H. Prince Salman
bin 'Abd al-'Aziz Al Saud

Foreword

Chevron Corporation has been doing business in Saudi Arabia for over 60 years. We obtained the concession from King Abdul Aziz in 1933 and spudded in the first oil well in 1938. We formed Aramco in 1944 and the rest is "history".

Chevron continues to conduct business in the Kingdom through its Arabian Chevron, Inc. office in Riyadh and our joint ventures with Saudi International Services Company and Saudi Chevron Petrochemical Company. We continue to search for and develop other opportunities to support the continued growth and economic welfare of the Kingdom.

Chevron is very pleased to be the sponsor of **Dir'iyyah and The First Saudi State,** by William Facey. We became involved in this project through a meeting with the publisher, Tom Stacey. The story is one that we have felt deserved full coverage and exposure not only to citizens of the Kingdom of Saudi Arabia but also to those of the Middle East and the rest of the world. We feel fortunate that our discussions with the publisher have resulted in such a splendid work.

The ruins of Dir'iyyah remain today, awaiting your inspection. We hope this book will bring the history of the ruins to life.

K. T. Derr

Kenneth T. Derr
Chairman of the Board
Chevron Corporation

Introduction

Superiority results from group feeling *('asabiyyah)*. Only by God's help in establishing His religion do individual desires come together in agreement ... and hearts become united. ... When hearts are turned towards the truth and reject the world and whatever is false, and advance towards God, they become one in their outlook. There are few differences. Mutual cooperation and support flourish. As a result the extent of the state widens, and the dynasty grows.

Ibn Khaldun (1332-1405 AD), *Muqaddimah* Chapter 3 section 4.
Translated by Franz Rosenthal.

The ruined city of Dir'iyyah, from 1745 until its fall in 1818 the capital of the First Saudi State, is the chief archaeological symbol of Saudi Arabian nationhood.

Its significance reaches far beyond its physical importance as a traditional Najdi capital. It stands for a society which, under the guidance of the teacher Shaykh Muhammad ibn 'Abd al-Wahhab and the first Imams of the House of Saud, attempted to purify what it saw as the decadent Islam of its day, and to embody the rule of God's law on earth. In this endeavour it was arguably more successful than any other Islamic community since the days of the Prophet himself. In propagating its message, it extended its sway over most of Arabia, including the Holy Cities of Makkah and Madinah.

This enterprise had far-reaching consequences for Arabian history. To establish a society based solely on the Shari'ah had profound implications, for Islamic religious thinking draws no distinction between religion, morality, law and politics. In spreading the message, the people of Dir'iyyah were creating a central authority which over-rode previous tribal divisions and feuds in the name of a higher ideal. The rule of law brought peace to the tribal scene in the desert and settlements. For a short time, a centralised state emerged which harnessed and harmonised tribal energies. The comparison with the first spread of Islam from Arabia in the 7th century AD is striking.

In the anarchic tribal context from which it emerged, many observers saw this reform movement, rightly, as a force for stability and progress. As the Anglo-Swiss explorer Burckhardt remarked in the early 19th century, it brought peace and prosperity to Najd, ending the constant feuding and introducing a system of centralised justice, to create a kind of "Bedouin commonwealth". Later in the century, the British regarded the movement as essentially civilising. Quite apart from the benefits of peace brought to tribes and settlements under the movement's sway, for foreign governments the formation of a state centred on Dir'iyyah or Riyadh greatly simplified the business of diplomatic contact.

For the people of Dir'iyyah, the function of human society and behaviour was to follow God's law, and to administer it the duty of the ruler. The state was not theocratic in the sense that the ruler was regarded as God's representative, with a divine right to rule and an infallible authority in the interpretation of divine law. The ruler was fallible, but was guided in his counsels by the learned religious scholars known as the *'ulama'*. In the First Saudi State based at Dir'iyyah (1745-1818), the ruler and the *'ulama'* achieved a striking harmony, based on equality, in the business of government. In the Second Saudi State based at Riyadh after 1824 this concept survived in theory but seems to have been progressively diluted in practice, as rulers became the dominant force in government. However, they continued to use the title of Imam, a term equally of religious and secular connotation.

Although portrayed as heretics by their Muslim opponents, the people of Dir'iyyah from the outset regarded themselves as ultra-orthodox Muslims seeking to purify Islam. They referred to themselves simply as "the Muslims", or else as *muwahhidun*, which can be translated literally but somewhat unsatisfactorily as "Unitarians". They were known to the outside world as Wahhabis, after their teacher. This started out as a term coined by their enemies and detractors, but has long since lost any derogatory connotation. It is a convenient term, and is occasionally used in this book.

The First Saudi State was brought to its knees by the destruction of Dir'iyyah in 1818, but its legacy passed to Riyadh in 1824 and remains very much alive in the Saudi Arabia of today. Despite the rapid modernisation of recent decades, the spirit of the reform movement remains fundamental to the nature of the Kingdom. The families of Shaykh Muhammad ibn 'Abd al-Wahhab and Muhammad ibn Saud have now determined the spiritual and political direction of Saudi society for almost 250 years, and their history remains intertwined with that of the modern state. To this day descendants of the Shaykh hold important posts in the government, and many members of the royal house trace their descent also from him.

A book devoted to the stirring topic of Dir'iyyah's rise and fall is long overdue. It combines a full description of the site itself which, together with its environs, has been specially photographed, with a description of the people and society which flourished there. Documentary evidence is drawn from the local Najdi chroniclers, such as Husayn ibn Ghannam and 'Uthman ibn Bishr, from European travellers and other Western accounts of the end of the 18th and early 19th centuries, and from Saudi and Western scholars. The history of Dir'iyyah is set against the background of the growth of settlement in Wadi Hanifah and the birth of the reform movement.

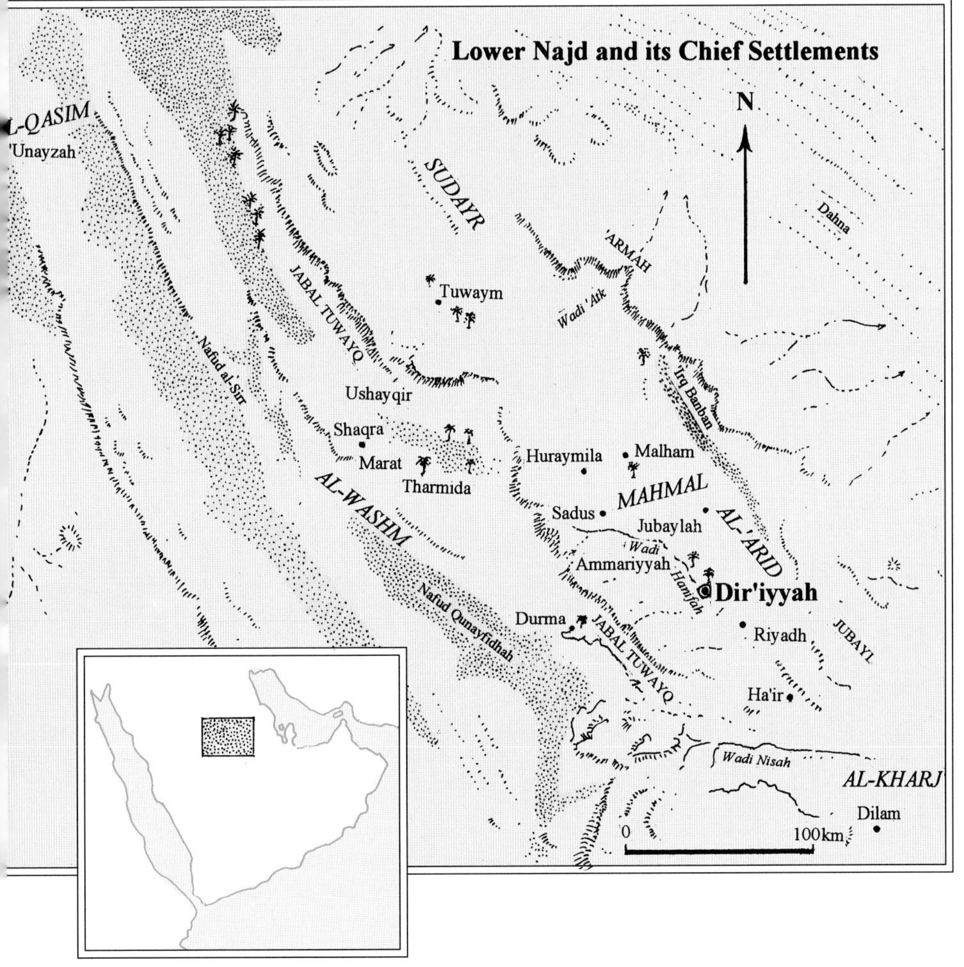

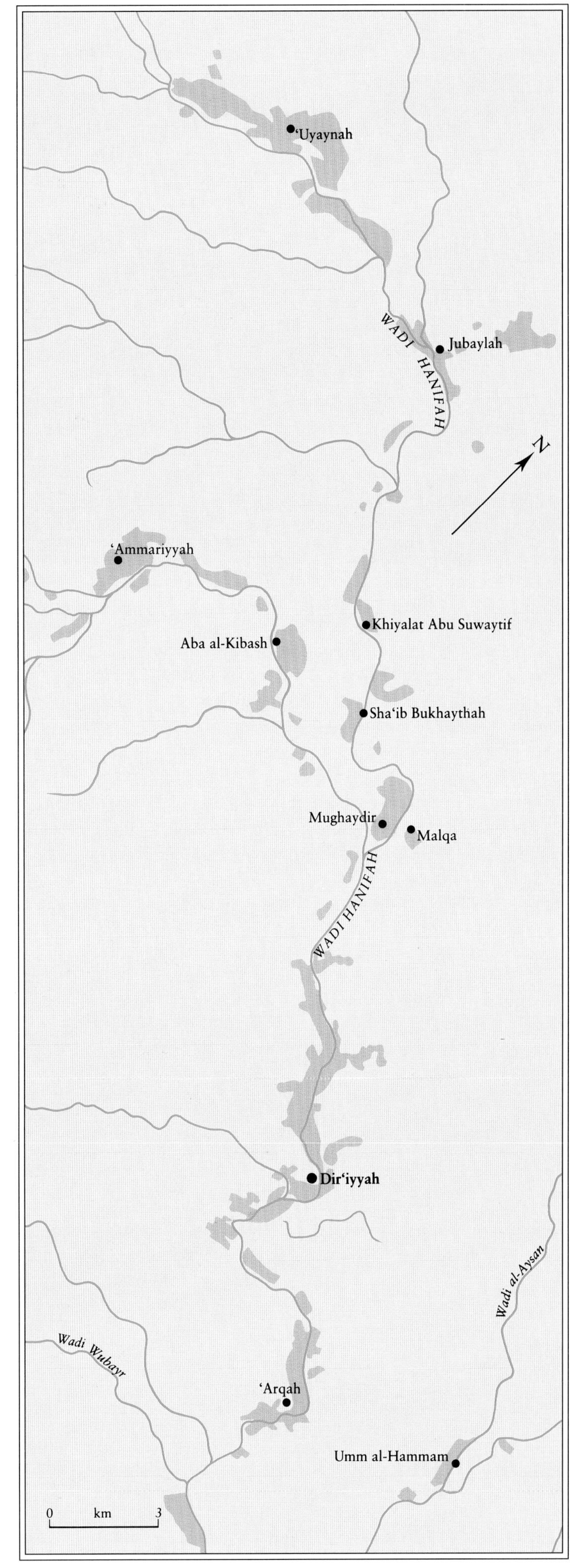

The wadi system and palm groves
in the vicinity of Dir'iyyah

CHAPTER ONE

The Land and its Fruits

Geography, climate and farming

NAJD AND WADI HANIFAH: GEOLOGY AND TOPOGRAPHY

Najd, meaning the highland plateau forming central Arabia, is a distinct geographical entity, surrounded by forbidding barriers isolating it from the outside world. Against expectations in such an arid land, Najd in its eastern part is a region of ancient settlement. Throughout history its people have been outstandingly self-sufficient. Despite isolation, they have exerted from time to time a profound influence on the surrounding regions.

Bounded by the great sand seas of the Nafud and Empty Quarter to north and south, Najd is separated from the Eastern Region and the Gulf coast by the long sand ridges of the Dahna. To the west the plateau ends in the mountain ranges of the Hijaz and Asir which run the length of western Arabia. Dir'iyyah and the Wadi Hanifah in which it is situated lie in the eastern part of Najd.

The topography of Najd is determined by the relief of the Arabian Peninsula as a whole. The igneous mountains of western Arabia – the Hijaz, Asir and Yemen – rise in ridges parallel to the Red Sea coast to, in places, 3000 metres and more. They form the watershed of Arabia: the rest of the Peninsula slopes gently downwards to the east, until the Arabian continental plate is subducted beneath the Iranian plate under the waters of the Gulf.

The drainage of Arabia is, hence, by a network of wadi systems which crosses Najd from west to east. These were carved, in wetter geological periods, by the action of water – a fact which, given Arabia's vegetation-free topography, is impressively clear from the air. Today they are dry wadis, but they still channel run-off water after the heavy desert rains, later retaining groundwater closer to the surface than in other areas. They provide important trans-peninsular routes, pasture areas and locations of settlement.

Once these wadi systems flowed together in Najd into three major rivers which reached the basin that today is filled by the Gulf. The courses of these rivers can still be discerned. In the north, Wadi al-Rumah/al-Batin drains al-Qasim and runs thence to the southern Euphrates. Wadi al-Sahba is formed by the confluence of the Wadi Hanifah, Wadi Nisah and others at al-Kharj, and drains towards the Sabkhat Matti and the Gulf coast just south-east of Qatar. The southernmost, Wadi al-Dawasir, is formed by the confluence of wadis at a major gap in the southern Jabal Tuwayq, and today drains into the Empty Quarter. Its waters drain beneath the sands into the Sabkhat Matti on the Gulf coast. These confluences and the large wadis which flow into them provide the most favourable areas for settlement and agriculture in Najd.

The great plateau of Najd slopes gently downwards from an average elevation of about 1100 metres in the west to about 600 metres in the east. Its eastern part is formed by a zone, some 250 kilometres wide and running north-south, of west-facing escarpments in resistant limestone, with plateaux on their eastern side which continue the gentle downward slope of Najd towards the east. The main one, the "backbone of Arabia", is Jabal Tuwayq, which runs from near the south-western end of the Empty Quarter, northwards towards Riyadh for some 650 kilometres. Then it turns north-westwards for almost 325 kilometres more, where it forms the western limit of Sudayr, and disappears into the Dahna sands just beyond Zilfi. In its central part, in the region of Riyadh, it rises in places to more than 1000 metres. Its cliffs can be awesome, commonly dropping 250 metres to the plain beneath. It is broken in

Above right: **The entire site of Turayf, the chief town and citadel of Dir'iyyah, from the north-east. The road runs along the bed of Wadi Hanifah. The settlement in the foreground is recent.**

Left: **The palm groves of Dir'iyyah flood readily after the torrential rains which relieve the aridity of Najd between two and fifteen times a year.**

DIR'IYYAH
AND
THE FIRST SAUDI STATE

Published by Stacey International
128 Kensington Church Street, London W8 4BH

Editor: Mark Petre
Assistant Editor: Kitty Carruthers
Photographer: Philip Hawkins
Art Director: John Fitzmaurice
Cartographer: Andras Bereznay
Translator: Megdi Ashmawi

British Library Cataloguing-in-Publication Data
A catalogue record for this book is available from the British Library

ISBN: 0905743 806

Printed and bound by Tien Wah Press, Singapore

The author and publisher wish to express special thanks to the following for their encouragement, guidance and help during the preparation of this work: HRH Prince Sultan bin Salman bin 'Abd al-'Aziz Al Saud, Raafat Al-Sabbagh, Dr Fahd al-Semmari, Dr Muhammad al-Sha'fi and Dr Zahir Othman.

The publishers are indebted to the following for additional pictures:
The British Museum: page 44 (*bottom*);
The Royal Geographical Society: pp. 72-3, 77 (*bottom*), 78 (*bottom*);
William Facey: p. 82 (*middle right*)

DIR'IYYAH
AND
THE FIRST SAUDI STATE

WILLIAM FACEY
PHOTOGRAPHY BY PHILIP HAWKINS

STACEY INTERNATIONAL

Half-title: The Palace of 'Umar ibn Saud rears imposingly over the Wadi Hanifah.

Title: The Palace of Sa'd ibn Saud is one of several structures recently restored by the Department of Antiquities and Museums.

This page: The west gate of Turayf, the chief town of the Dir'iyyah oasis, gives onto the main east-west street passing the Palace of Sa'd ibn Saud.

Contents

places by passes, such as the Haysiyyah pass near the source of Wadi Hanifah above 'Uyaynah.

The other, lesser escarpments run parallel to Jabal Tuwayq, principally its northern section, and on either side of it. Notable to the east and north-east of Riyadh are the Jubayl and 'Armah escarpments. Wadi Hanifah drains the plateau of Jabal Tuwayq, and runs south-eastwards into the depression between it and the escarpments of 'Armah and Jubayl to its east. It has fostered a succession of historic towns such as Jubaylah, 'Uyaynah, Dir'iyyah, Manfuhah and Riyadh. This district is traditionally known as al-'Arid.

Between the escarpments, and parallel to them, lie great *nafud*s or sand strips. The Nafud al-Sirr/Nafud al-Dahi system runs almost the length of Jabal Tuwayq to the west. Between it and the northern section of Jabal Tuwayq lie the Nafud al-Thuwayrat and Nafud Qunayfidah sand strips. Beneath the 'Armah escarpment lies the sand strip of 'Irq Banban, a favourite pasture and hunting resort for the people of Wadi Hanifah.

This region of escarpments and sand strips forming the eastern part of Najd is known as Safilat Najd, or Lower Najd. Plains and depressions have formed in the tracts between the low, down-sloping eastern reaches of each plateau and the cliff of the next escarpment. It is here that the *nafud*s have been formed by wind-blown sand. Many of the wadi systems of central Arabia discharge their floods into these plains, forming catchment areas of alluvial soils, or *rawdat*, which are suitable for grazing, and sometimes farming and settlement. In such areas ground-water is close to the surface and can be reached easily by wells, so ensuring availability of water all year round for both *badu* and settlers.

Lower Najd is composed of relatively recent sedimentary formations of marine origin in the Mesozoic and early Tertiary eras: limestone, sandstone, shale, gravel and sand tracts. The soft rock formations are easily eroded by weathering and water, and broken down into silts by the action of floods carried down through the wadis towards the flood plains and depressions. Since the beginnings of oasis agriculture, perhaps during the third millennium BC, the wadis and silt depressions of Lower Najd have supported agricultural settlements on their terraces, bays, flood plains and depressions, and sometimes even in the torrent bed itself.

As Wadi Hanifah descends it collects the waters from many tributaries, which wash down fertile sediments into its bed. In the area of Dir'iyyah several such tributaries cut through the limestone massif to join the wadi, the largest of them being Sha'ib Safar, which joins Wadi Hanifah opposite the fertile plot of Mulaybid at the southern end of Dir'iyyah. Wadi Hanifah itself cuts a deep course through the limestone in places, leaving cliffs on either side. At the base of these cliffs, and at the mouths of the tributaries, the silts form valuable farming land, and here are to be found the plantations and irrigated field systems of the settlers. Wadi Hanifah's lower reaches, beyond Riyadh and before it joins Wadi Nisah, are particularly suitable for settlement. Lower down still, to the south-east, it joins Wadi Nisah after the latter has broken through the Tuwayq range. Here lies the fertile, low-lying district of al-Kharj.

Lower Najd is distinct from 'Aliyat Najd, or Upper Najd, to its west. Here the surface formations are of much older geological origin. Upper Najd extends westward from the westernmost sand strip, the Nafud al-Sirr, to the mountains of western Arabia and forms, with them, the Arabian Shield: a region of ancient igneous and metamorphic rock. On the plateau of Upper Najd this is relatively level, broken only by isolated rock outcrops and mountains. The wadis are small and relatively shallow, as they are closer to the watershed and the network has not converged into major wadis. The gravelly soil is thin but widespread. Unsuitable for agriculture, it provides excellent grazing after rain, and so has been dominated by the great nomadic bedouin tribes.

Above: **The wadis feeding into Wadi Hanifah are dry for most of the year, but support a sparse vegetation.**

Above right: **The upper reach of Wadi Hanifah near 'Uyaynah.**

Right: **Lakes form after heavy rain in Sha'ib Safar, a major tributary of Wadi Hanifah which runs into Dir'iyyah at its southern end.**

CLIMATE AND RAINFALL

Najd forms part of the arid belt which includes the Sahara Desert and the entire Arabian Peninsula apart from its south-western and south-eastern corners. Of all the large countries on earth, Saudi Arabia is perhaps the driest. Its traditional settled communities have faced and overcome an extreme challenge to survival. Najd has a long, hot and almost totally dry summer. Temperatures can reach 48°C, the average in July being 34.8°C. The cloudless skies, and the fact that it is far removed from the moderating effects of the sea, mean that temperature can vary sharply between night and day, and between summer and winter. However, the perceived effect of both heat and cold is mitigated by the low humidity. In winter the average January temperature is 15°C, but this conceals the fact that hard frosts can occur, causing severe damage to crops. The lowest temperature recorded is -7°C.

By the time that winds reach central Arabia they have been deprived of most of their moisture, and therefore rainfall is very low. During the summer, the prevailing wind comes from the south, and is totally dry. During the winter the cold, dry *shamal* blows from the north, from central Asia. The *shamal* is offset in late winter by depressions tracking from the eastern Mediterranean. These winds bear the meagre rainfall of Najd, including the most valued, the *wasmi* rains of spring which dramatically revive desert vegetation.

Average annual rainfall around Dir'iyyah, at 117mm, is well below the annual amount of 250mm above which dry farming would begin to be possible. Were it not for the availability of ground-water which, by animal-drawn wells, traditionally supplied water for irrigation and daily needs the year round, permanent settlement on any scale in Lower Najd would have been as inconceivable as it has been in Upper Najd.

The rainfall averages are misleading as they conceal the great irregularity of rainfall in Najd. It is extremely erratic, not only from year to year but within the period when rain can be most reasonably expected to fall, that is in the short winter and spring from December to April. It can range from just 15mm recorded in 1966 to the 257mm recorded ten years later. The rain that does fall is typical of desert rainfall: it tends to arrive in the form of violent rainstorms and heavy showers of short duration. Half or more of a year's rainfall may fall in a single day. Such downpours can be very localised.

Camels graze in the sands between al-Washm and al-'Arid *(left)*, and crop the richer vegetation in the bed of the northern Wadi Hanifah *(right)*.

To settlements in their path, they can also be as devastating as drought: rainfall funnelling through the wadi systems can produce cataclysmic floods which have been known to sweep away entire settlements. Wadi Hanifah receives on average four or five such floods in winter and spring, sometimes as late as May. In a bad year there may be only two, while an exceptional season may bring up to fifteen.

GEOGRAPHY, CLIMATE AND TRADITIONAL SOCIETY IN NAJD

Geography and climate do not, on their own, determine the nature of societies. But they do impose limits on what traditional societies can achieve in material terms. With the domestication of the camel and date palm during the long centuries before 1000 BC, a tribal society of nomads and settlers emerged in Najd which was uniquely adapted to some of the harshest physical conditions on earth. Their material resources were meagre and precarious, and economic opportunity very low. They have survived through robust self-sufficiency, in isolation from the outside world.

The pattern of drought and plenty profoundly affected their economic and social development. Periods of relative growth and prosperity have been cut short by severe droughts, some lasting a single year, more devastating ones lasting three or four. With the drying up of wells farming has become impossible. The resulting famine, malnutrition and disease has caused emigration to other parts and wholesale death of settled populations within their towns and villages. The meagreness of resources meant that survival was possible only in scattered small groups, relying on strong solidarity within to maintain themselves against competition from without.

Drought and disease are a recurring theme in the chronicles of the traditional historians of Najd. Drought has frequently brought on

periods of political upheaval, as settled communities competed among themselves or with the bedouin for diminishing resources. This process was often exacerbated by the divided nature of Najdi society itself, organised as it was on a tribal basis into separate competing settlements with no strong central authority. The emergence of the reform movement of the great Shaykh Muhammad ibn 'Abd al-Wahhab at Dir'iyyah in the mid-18th century wrought a profound change in this respect, as local loyalties were replaced by a wider one to religion and state. The energies previously consumed by internal competition were re-directed outwards, with results which astonished the outside world.

The isolation of Najd, the poverty of its resources and the aridity of its climate have generally combined to make it an unattractive prospect for invaders. It has on occasion been claimed by outsiders, for example by the Abbasids, the Ottomans, the rulers of al-Hasa or the Sharifs of Makkah. But the claim has seldom been implemented and then not for long. On the whole it has been left to tribal control or local rulers. As one local chronicler pithily remarked: "Najd is like the Chinese proverb: if there are many soldiers in it, they become hungry, and if there are few, then they perish."

AGRICULTURE AND LIVESTOCK

Nowhere in Arabia, with the exception of the highlands of the south-west and parts of Oman, is rainfall adequate to support rain-fed agriculture. Groundwater is the key to survival, as much for the bedouin as for settlers. But with hard work, the Najdi farmer could flourish, provided that there was stability in the settlement and the wells did not dry up.

From the earliest times farming was almost totally dependent on irrigation from groundwater sources, where these were near the surface in the wadi systems and silt flats. The settlements of Lower Najd depended on great

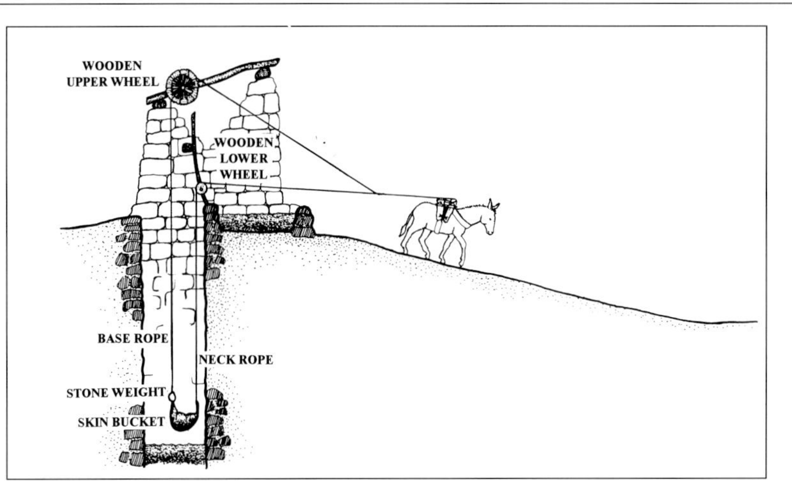

A working well is maintained for the public on the edge of Wadi Hanifah, just outside the walls of Turayf *(far left, left top, left and above)*. The mechanism *(above right)* is an ancient one; without it, cultivation in Najd would have been impossible.

Fields at Mulaybid *(below and right)* at the southern end of the Dir'iyyah oasis are today irrigated from wells using diesel pumps. The earth-banked channels still used to distribute the water are ancient.

An aqueduct *(above)* **leads water from a channel running along the edge of the gardens below the cliff of Wadi Hanifah.**

The gardens of Dir'iyyah were always a paradise of shade, greenery and flowing water, supporting a rich bird and insect life *(left, above right and far right).*

stone-lined wells dug down to the water table. Animal power was used to draw the water up. This is an ancient system, and the evolution of the Najdi animal-draw well probably goes hand-in-hand with the evolution of oasis agriculture and date palm cultivation in central Arabia, which perhaps reaches back to the third millennium BC.

Well-digging was normally done on a cooperative basis, with neighbours and relatives helping without payment. In the recent past at least, the depth of wells in Wadi Hanifah was commonly about twenty metres, judging from the length of surviving donkey ramps. This was quite shallow by central Arabian standards. In Dir'iyyah's heyday the water table may have been even closer to the surface.

The operation of the well (*saniya*, pl. *sawani*), in the Dir'iyyah gardens, was done by donkeys and mules. Unless the winter rains

were plentiful, irrigation of cereal crops would have to begin immediately after ploughing and sowing, at the end of the autumn but before the winter rains, which started usually in December. It would then have to continue for the next five months, the work becoming increasingly hard, as the crops grew and the heat increased, until the harvest in late April. Then, during the summer months, irrigation of the date palm gardens, with their associated crops of fodder (alfalfa), vegetables and fruit trees, had to continue. The creaking and whining of the well wheels, day and night, was noted by many visitors as the constant background music to life in the Najdi settlements. Distribution of the water was by unlined channels, and so wastage was considerable, limiting the size of gardens, which tended to be usually of not more than one hectare.

The date palm was crucial to subsistence, not just as the staple source of food, fuel, fodder and raw material for household items and building, but because it provided the environment in which many other plants could be grown, most especially vegetables and fruits – many of which can thrive only in the partial shade within or next to palm plantations. Date palms have a high salt tolerance and hence were well adapted to local conditions.

Next in importance were the cereal crops – wheat, barley and millet (*dhurra* – sorghum, guinea corn; and *dukhn* – pearl or bulrush millet) – whose cultivation in Arabia is as old as oasis farming. Wheat and barley, as well as being grown on irrigated land, were also sown on low-lying silt flats outside the irrigated area but within easy reach of the settlement. The area varied from season to season: good rains encouraged an expansion

of the area. The Wadi Hanifah settlements had ploughs made of wood, sometimes with an iron tongue to break the soil, and were used to plough in the wheat and barley grain after manuring and sowing. Millet was grown as a summer crop within the irrigated area.

Alfalfa or lucerne was the chief crop after dates, wheat and barley. Vivid green open plots of alfalfa were a common sight among the palm groves. It could be cut three or four times a year provided it was well irrigated after cutting. Vital as fodder, it was used principally to feed the camels, horses and cows belonging to the townsfolk.

It is thought that the Muslim conquests of North Africa, Spain and Sicily introduced the Arabs to some of the vegetables and fruits which were later disseminated into central Arabia, such as apricots, peaches, watermelons and aubergines, while Arab traders introduced Seville oranges, limes and lemons from India into Oman during the Middle Ages. During the entire Islamic period new varieties of fruit and vegetables were being introduced into Najd, so providing an increasingly varied diet. The latest to be introduced must have been species originating in the Americas, such as tomatoes, maize and squashes. Vegetable gardens were found within the date gardens, generally occupying the space between the date palms. Fruit trees might be planted in small orchards or along the edges of date groves. Vegetables and fruit were only grown on a limited scale, for the family's own use.

Most of the garden produce which the British explorer and Arabist Harry St. John Philby found to be well established in southern Najd in the early 20th century, had probably already been cultivated there for at least three centuries and in most cases very much longer: onions, beans, aubergines, cucumbers, okra, cotton bushes, figs, grapes, peaches, apricots, a small apple, pomegranates,

The great outer fortification wall of the Dir'iyyah oasis *(above)* **protects now, as before a flourishing system of cultivation in which crops and other produce are grown in the shade of the date-palms** *(right and far right).*

mulberries, melons, lemons and the large thick-skinned citrus known locally as *tranj*. Garlic has certainly also been grown for a very long time. In the spaces in between the women would plant herbs and spices such as coriander, fenugreek, peppergrass, cumin and safflower, which were used in the preparation not only of food but also of medicines and cosmetics.

The other major tree of the Najdi settlement was the *ithl* or tamarisk, whose feathery foliage is still a familiar sight today. It is very easy to grow, requiring surface water only during its first year, afterwards putting down a long taproot to the water table. Its uses were many, for roof timbers, carpentry, firewood and dune stabilisation.

As for livestock, settlers kept small flocks of goats and sheep which they entrusted to goatherds during the day. Most families had a cow of the small humped variety which they kept for milk in an enclosure by the house. A few camels were kept in the settlements for carrying and riding. In times of military emergency camels would have to be brought in from the desert. Horses were highly prized and were kept only by the well-to-do, usually members of the ruling family, although during Dir'iyyah's years of prosperity many ordinary citizens also prided themselves on being able to keep a horse.

Above: The Dir'iyyah oasis was dotted with villages, hamlets and farmhouses, like this old one, among the palms.

Right: A typical mix of date-palms, tamarisk and fruit trees, with an abandoned farmhouse, at Mulaybid. Today vegetables are grown commercially in open plots like this, irrigated by diesel pumps. In the old days, a few vegetables were grown within and on the edge of the palms for family consumption.

A flock of goats *(left)* is kept by the herdsman within the walls of this historic old fort in the Bulayda area.

Right: Najdi goats are a tough, adaptable and ancient breed with no qualms about posing for the camera.

Tamarisk trees *(left)* are grown in all Najdi oases. Their wood *(right)* is light and tough, and their straight trunks and branches made them ideal for the construction of Dir'iyyah.

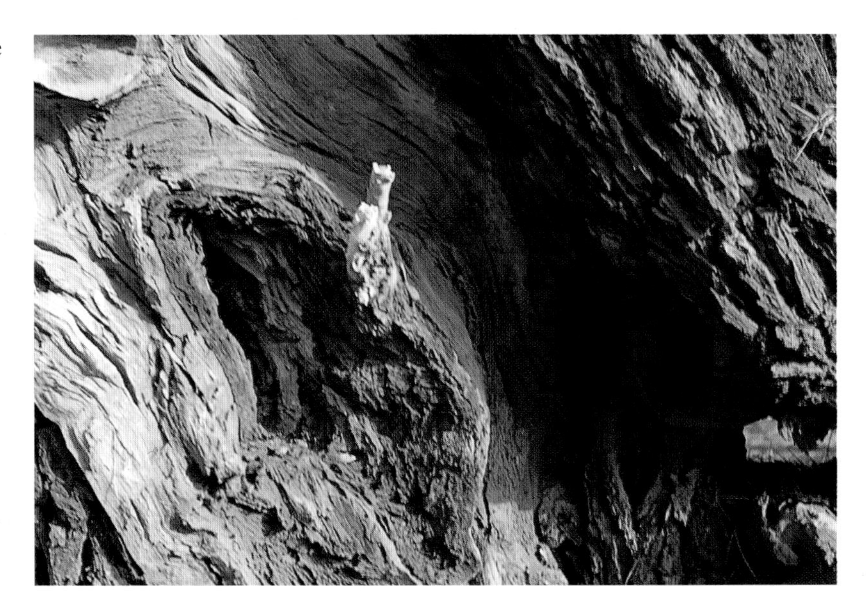

Right: Vivid green plots of alfalfa *(barsim)*, like this one by Nazlat al-Nasiriyyah, are a common sight in Najdi oases today. Grown for fodder, alfalfa is highly nutritious and, if properly irrigated, can produce four crops a year.

Below: The small tributary wadis leading to the Wadi Hanifah provide rich alluvial soil. This one is the first to cut through the heights just to the west of Turayf.

CHAPTER TWO

Settlers and Nomads

Early life in Wadi Hanifah

THE RE-SETTLEMENT OF WADI HANIFAH

Tradition has it that Dir'iyyah was founded in AD 1446. But before we come to the story of its foundation, we must first consider the general social and economic setting in Lower Najd in which it took place. From all the evidence it seems that the 15th century marked the start of a gradual re-growth of settlement in Lower Najd. During the centuries that went before, the settlements that existed had declined and Najd was dominated by the bedouin tribes. This process had begun during the 9th century AD. Before that time, there had been a prevailing settled culture centred on Hajr al-Yamamah, located in the area of present-day Riyadh.

Hajr had a long history. Its foundation was ascribed to the semi-legendary pre-Islamic tribe of Jadis, and it had been taken over, perhaps in the 5th century AD, by the influential tribe of Banu Hanifah, whose name lives on in Wadi Hanifah on which Dir'iyyah was to be founded. Banu Hanifah were originally part of the nomadic Bakr ibn Wa'il group of tribes, but in settling at Hajr and Khidrimah in al-Kharj they established themselves as rulers of the important region of al-Yamamah. Their leaders such as Hawdha ibn Ali and Musaylama played colourful roles in the history of this part of Arabia up to the dawn of Islam in the 7th century AD.

Hajr al-Yamamah flourished during the early centuries of Islam, until the power of the Abbasid dynasty in Iraq began to dwindle towards the end of the 9th century AD. The lean centuries after AD 900 found it in reduced circumstances, but it seems to have survived as a community. By the time of Ibn Battutah's visit in 1331-2, there were signs of revival. He described it as "a fine and fertile city with running streams and trees, inhabited by different clans of Arabs, most of whom are of the Banu Hanifah, this being their land from of old. Their amir is Tufayl ibn Ghanim. I continued my journey from there in the company of this amir to make the pilgrimage ... and so came to Makkah."

However, it is to the following century that the sources ascribe the beginnings of a widespread re-population and foundation of settlements in Lower Najd. A factor in this was certainly an improvement in climate in the middle of the 15th century which continued until the early decades of the 17th century. There had also been a revival in the commerce of the Gulf. This was the golden age of the trade of Hormuz with the East, and the great centres of the Eastern Province, al-Hasa and Qatif, were flourishing under the devout amirs of the Jabrid dynasty.

As a general rule the towns of Lower Najd were established or revived not by their original inhabitants, but by newcomers from within Najd. The old tribe of Tamim who, like Banu Hanifah, had exchanged their nomadic life in the pre-Islamic era for a settled existence, were especially active in colonising new settlements. Coming from al-Washm and villages in Sudayr, Tamim grew in number and immigrated to Wadi Hanifah and al-Qasim, where they either established new towns or joined existing ones. To them 'Uyaynah owed its origins, its site being bought by a Tamimi in the mid-15th century from Al Yazid of Banu Hanifah. Other major settlements of the Tamim in Lower Najd were Tharmida, Ushayqir in al-Washm, and Rawdah in Sudayr.

The growth of the settlements owed something also to nomadic tribesmen, particularly after the decline of Jabrid influence in Najd soon after AD 1500. Throughout the three hundred years before the reform movement in the 18th century, successive waves of nomads were attracted into Lower Najd, largely it seems by the general improvement in the climate in the later 15th and 16th centuries. A problem of overpopulation ensued, which was exacerbated by a series of droughts in the 17th century. The people's response was to resort to either settlement, if they were nomads, or to emigration, which both nomads and settlers might try.

In the face of these trends, the Banu Hanifah were on the whole unable to maintain or increase their dominant role in the population. Instead, they tended to be swallowed up by the newcomers. In the 14th century Al Yazid, who are thought to have been a remnant of Banu Hanifah, are recorded as having still been in control of the old settlements, perhaps by then little more than villages, of Wadi Hanifah, Wadi Qurran and al-Kharj. In the 15th century Al Yazid still retained control of the Wadi Hanifah to the north up to Jubaylah, including the settlements of Wusayl and Na'amiyyah. But favoured areas within the Banu Hanifah territory, such as 'Uyaynah and Dir'iyyah, were not being utilised for settlement and farming. The sale of the unoccupied area of what was to become 'Uyaynah, the largest town in Najd in the 17th century, to a Tamimi at this time, shows how far Banu Hanifah's numbers and influence had

declined. By the 16th century Hajr had lost its dominance and was splitting up into a number of small villages such as Mi'kal and Muqrin, later to be absorbed into Riyadh.

It was an awareness of Banu Hanifah's decline which persuaded Ibn Dir', the chief of the Hanafi clan of Al Dir' who ruled Hajr and Jiz'ah, to invite his relatives of the Muradah clan of the Duru', who were then living on the Gulf coast, to come and settle within his domain. Thus, in 1446, was Dir'iyyah founded, and we shall turn to this story in the next chapter. It was a successful move, and the Muradah clan was eventually to produce the most powerful and prosperous ruling house in Arabia's history, the House of Saud.

The rest of Banu Hanifah fared less well. By the 17th century only two settlements apart from Dir'iyyah are reported to have been ruled by families who traced their origins to Banu Hanifah: Manfuhah and Muqrin. By the 18th century there remained only a few families of Hanafi origin in these towns. The most prominent were Al Zar'ah, Al Mudayris, Al Suhaym and Al Dughaythir of Riyadh, and the Julalil and Al Sha'lan of Manfuhah.

Alluvial mud washed down by heavy winter and spring storms dries out quickly into fantastic delicate patterns *(above and below)*. **Many species of plant, both annual and perennial, are adapted to aridity and burst into bloom after rain** *(left)*.

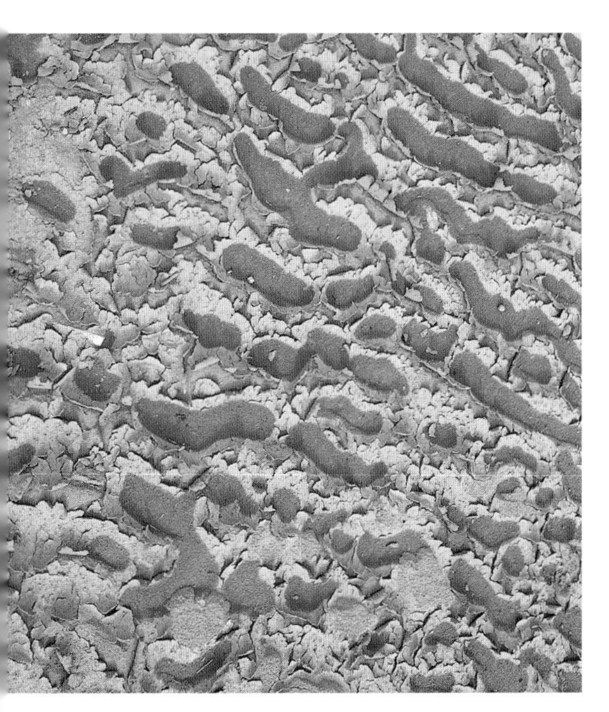

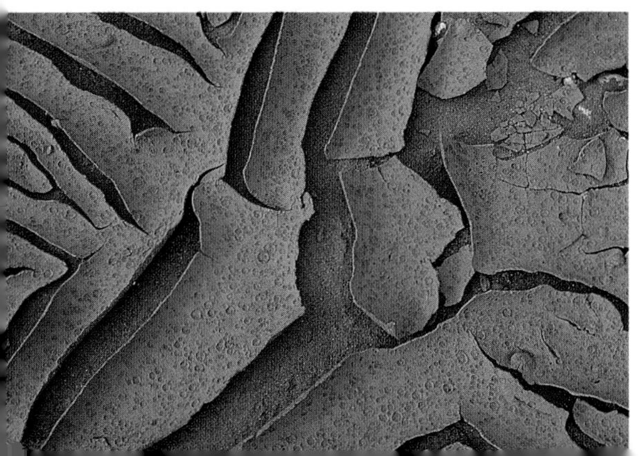

SOCIAL STRUCTURE IN THE TOWNS

The pattern of settlement in these early times tended to be scattered. It is in the nature of tribal social organisation that each lineage group tends to segment and assert its independence as a clan. A successful clan will then compete for overlordship of tribe or settlement. Within Arabian towns it might often happen that solidarity within each tribal and lineage division would lead them to live as a separate group, just as nomadic families and lineage groups stick together in the desert, with the result that a single settlement could comprise two or more quite distinct units. These might often be heavily fortified and permanently at odds with each other. Nor would they be above enlisting outside forces in alliance against their internal rivals. On a less crystallised level, groups of fluctuating composition within a settlement would be in a state of constant rivalry, each with the aim of imposing its own rule.

Hence many Najdi towns were in a state of continual upheaval as rival groups strove to outdo each other. Without a larger vision than one provided by the tribal system itself, the pre-eminence of one group over another tended to be brief. This instability was the bane of human existence until the reform movement at Dir'iyyah in the 18th century.

By the time of Dir'iyyah's foundation in the mid-15th century, the pattern of society that characterised the Najdi towns until the modern era seems already to have been fixed. The settled people were divided into three classes: the *qabiliyyun* (sing. *qabili*) or tribesmen, the Banu Khadir or *khadiriyyun* (sing. *khadiri*), and the *'abid* or slaves.

Those families who were able to trace their ancestry to one of the recognised Arab tribes, whether nomadic, partly settled or fully settled, like the Tamim, formed the *qabiliyyun*. Most of the settled people were *qabiliyyun*, and to them belonged the rulers of the settlements as well as most of the social prestige.

A smaller number of the settled people could not identify their tribal origins. These were the *khadiriyyun*. It can be argued that they represented various earlier phases of tribal settlement, going back to ancient times; with time, their tribal affiliation had grown weak and was eventually forgotten. Even in the old settlements they were inferior both numerically and socially to the *qabiliyyun*. One can deduce from this that the latest waves of settlement, which occurred in the 15th-17th centuries, were numerically in terms of the re-population of the Najdi settlements.

The *khadiriyyun* were in general productive, working as farmers and traders – both occupations respected among the *qabiliyyun*. They were also artisans, pursuing crafts and trades which were considered menial by the *qabiliyyun*. In this, it seems that they were more adapted to the needs of urban existence than the more recently arrived *qabiliyyun*, who maintained some of their bedouin attitudes towards urban occupations. This further supports the view that the *khadiriyyun* formed an earlier settled stratum than the *qabiliyyun* within the towns.

Finally there were the *'abid*, or slaves. These constituted the smallest settled class and were of African origin. Slaves were kept by rulers and wealthy families, both nomadic and sedentary, as household servants and retainers. They might often reach positions of power and responsibility as their chiefs' representatives within settlements. In Najd, slaves were emancipated after a certain time.

The Najdi town was ruled by its shaykh or *ra'is*, who was drawn from its chief family. This family, known as the *shuyukh* (sing. *shaykh*) or *ru'asa'* (sing. *ra'is*), owed its right to rule to having founded the settlement. Alternatively it might emerge after the founding of the settlement, by usurping the descendants of the founders or their successors.

Right of succession to the rulership usually passed to the eldest son of the previous ruler. However, this was by no means obligatory, and in practice any brother, son or cousin might assert himself either by persuading the influential members of the family of his superior shaykhly qualities, or by force. This indeterminacy in matters of succession meant that different branches of the ruling clan often staked competing claims to the chieftainship, and so was one of the main causes of strife within Najdi settlements. In fact, the larger the ruling clan grew, the more segmented it became, so increasing the likelihood of such a state of affairs.

The power of the *ru'asa'* was rooted in ownership. They were regarded, by virtue of having founded the settlement, as the rightful owners of its land, water resources and the reserved grazing areas (*himas*) around it. Hence, the property of the settlement was the shaykh's to dispose of by sale, lease or grant to whomever he chose. The perennial preoccupations of the ruler were the defence and survival of his settlement, and the increase of his clan's influence at the expense of rivals within or outside the settlement. In practice this meant that the ruler's right to dispose of land was used to expand his power base by inviting new settlers upon whose support he could count, whether they were from his own tribe or outside it. This also increased the ruler's revenues.

While much of the land was cultivated by the *ru'asa'* using employed or slave labour, the rest was ceded to others in various ways. Some might simply be given away, as a means of attracting new settlers. Another common arrangement was share-cropping, the owner taking a share according to whether or not the land was already planted and whether or not a well already existed. In the case of virgin land, the share-cropping contract would be long-term, perhaps even for several hundred years. Land might also be leased, again for up to several hundred years. The long-term nature of such contracts could cause problems with the passage of generations, for example if the lessees became more prosperous than the owners, or if the owners after several generations came to covet the land developed by the lessees.

Those who settled after the original founders were attracted to the settlement by the protection offered by the *ru'asa'* and the agricultural or trading opportunities there. These settlers were known as the *jiran* (sing. *jar*, literally neighbour). There was a basic symbiosis between *ru'asa'* and *jiran*, in which the *ru'asa'* undertook to protect persons and property in exchange for military service and a share of the *jiran*'s crops. The basis of society was, hence, a local kind of feudal system, in which land tenure was bound up with military service and a tax in kind. The share of the *jiran*'s crops was collected by the ruler at harvest time. The proportion collected is not known, but amounts of 50% and 25% are recorded. It seems to have varied from settlement to settlement, and to have depended to some extent on the relationship of the settler to the ruler.

In addition there was a sales tax, which was collected in kind and which was levied on goods sold and trade passing through, and a tax imposed on pilgrims as payment for protection. At times when raids or campaigns were being planned, an extra levy was imposed in kind in order to bring in supplies.

As the *'ulama'*, or religious advisers, grew more influential, the religious tax or *zakah* began to be levied, the idea being that it should replace the ruler's previous sources of tax revenue. This led in many cases to resistance by rulers to the introduction of Shari'ah law. *Zakah* was levied on grain, dates and livestock, and might be either taken in kind or sold by the ruler's agents, the cash being deposited in the *bayt al-mal* (treasury).

Tax revenues were ostensibly to enable the ruler to maintain the town's defences and to provide for other matters of common interest. In practice much of the income was distributed among the members of the *ru'as'a* , who felt that, as descendants of the founder, it was part of their rightful inheritance. The basis of distribution could itself become a matter of dispute among them.

As with feudalism elsewhere, the system in the Najdi towns could operate to the benefit or disadvantage of the inhabitants. Rulers might exploit their *jiran* by trying to extort the maximum amount that they thought they could bear, and fail to fulfil their obligations towards them. By contrast the best rulers, in the words of the Najdi poet and satirist Humaydan al-Shuway'ir, were:

> ... like the lion that protects his realm and refuses to be trodden upon. They protect their subjects against robbers and raiders. They take the initiative against their enemies, whether nomads or settlers, in order to keep their domain prosperous. They are sweet to friends and sour to enemies. Whenever bedouins tread on them, they cast their corpses on the open field. They are passionate and defend their *jiran* with all their abilities. It is those who give harmony [*to their people*] and gain respect from them.

The idea of the just ruler was a powerful one in the Najdi settlements. Public opinion and respect were all-important in the maintenance of the ruler's position, just as it was for the shaykh of the nomadic tribe. His authority was by no means absolute: it depended on his personality, good reputation and ability to persuade. In reaching decisions, therefore, he had always to take into consideration the interests of the *ru'as'a* and *jiran*, and the consensus of his *'ulama'* , if they existed in the settlement. As among the nomads, the ruler's authority was based on the consent of the people. If they lost respect for his judgments or behaviour, they would support an alternative claimant who they felt would better represent their interests. The main difference between a nomadic tribal shaykh and the chief of a settlement was that the latter's position was reinforced by the property ownership of his tribal group.

As the influence of Islam deepened in the larger Najdi settlements throughout the period up till the emergence of the reform movement, so the image of the just ruler was reinforced and the ruler's decisions became increasingly conditioned by considerations of Islamic justice and consensus as represented to him by the *'ulama'*. Customary law was, however, the basis of government in the settlements throughout most of this period. The ruler might do double duty as judge (*qadi*) in the town or, alternatively, some other eminent and respected figure might fulfil this role. As the influence of the reform movement grew in the early 18th century, several rulers were to find that the judgments of a *qadi* of the Shari'ah law posed an unacceptable threat to their own authority. In these circumstances the *qadi* might move on to another settlement.

In enforcing his judgments the ruler could rely on no formally established executive arm. In practice, however, he employed a bodyguard, which consisted of slaves and freeborn retainers. The richer he was, the more he could afford. The freeborn retainers might be either settlers or nomads seeking employment. As a permanent body of trained fighting men, the ruler's bodyguard was an important social and political element in the Najdi towns, combining the roles of police, regular soldiers and administrative officers of the shaykh – in effect, the enforcement agency of central authority.

THE NOMADIC AND SEMI-NOMADIC TRIBES

Nomadic tribes in Najd could be divided into true nomads and semi-nomads. Of the two the true nomads were the most mobile and the most powerful. Their wealth, mobility and fighting qualities were based on their ownership of camel herds and some horses. They regarded themselves as *asil* or noble, and disdained those belonging to tribes which had no component of true nomads.

All nomads were economically dependent on the towns for various essential supplies, but they tended to visit them only once a year, at harvest time. They would spend eight months of the year, from September till June, on the move, in search of pasture. During the summer months they would congregate at desert wells under their control. In their annual wanderings in search of pasture they generally kept to their own tribal territory, or *dirah*. Some *dirah*s covered vast areas of Najd, and might include the *dirah*s of lesser tribes. In times of failing rainfall they might have to move on, while at other times they might be displaced by another tribe. These movements generally occurred in a south-west to north-east direction across Najd, resulting in the familiar age-old pattern of tribes immigrating into the Syrian desert and borders of Iraq.

True bedouin in the sense of prizing their freedom from outside control above all else, they were as self-sufficient as it is possible to be in the desert. Their spirit of independence made them scornful of those willing to endure the more circumscribed, if more productive, conditions of settled life. Yet the nomads could also be quick to change their lifestyle and settle if they saw an economic advantage in so doing. Recent history has shown how adaptable the bedouin are in adjusting to changed circumstances. Membership of the tribe often spanned the entire spectrum of nomads, semi-nomads and settlers. Once they settled, however, as during the 15th century and after, they might keep many of their old attitudes, which explains why they continued to look down upon certain trades and to value others, such as transport services, disproportionately.

Nomadic warrior aristocracies might extend their power over the towns, as happened with the Shammar of Hail in the 19th century. The towns on the other hand, when they were strong, would seek not only to defend their territories and grazing grounds from the nomads, but bring them into alliance and even make them tributary. Nomad and settler tended to see themselves in a state of permanent competition, but this in fact masked an underlying economic interdependence which was even more important.

The semi-nomads were less numerous, less mobile and poorer than the true nomads, with whom nonetheless they often shared tribal affiliation. They were primarily sheep- and goat-herders. The term semi-nomadism in fact covers many degrees of livestock-dependent lifestyle, from primarily nomadic pastoralists, who owned some camels and were less dependent on farming, to semi-sedentary pastoralists who were simply the herding off-shoot of a mainly settled agricultural community. At their most dependent, herdsmen might simply be a minority group employed by settlers to look after livestock on the more or less distant pastures over which the settlement claimed grazing rights. Such pastures were known as *hima*s, or reserved areas, and the claimant settlement's rights might be disputed by its nomadic or settled neighbours as its influence waned. Semi-nomads and semi-sedentaries roamed the wadis and silt flats of Lower Najd within easy reach of the towns – a situation unlike that in Upper Najd, where settlements were small and few, and which was dominated by the true camel nomads.

RELATIONS BETWEEN NOMAD AND SETTLER

In Lower Najd economic pressures and kinship ties with settlers brought about a constant interchange between settlers and semi-nomads. As the settled *qabiliyyun* were of nomadic or semi-nomadic origin, tribal ties between pastoralists and their settled kin were often close. Kinship could create common political interests. Coalitions of nomads and settlers often formed across the nomad/settler divide to oppose other alliance groups.

In addition, nomad and townsman were economically dependent upon one another in certain fundamental ways. The nomadic bedouin family depended on its herds or flocks for its daily sustenance and much of

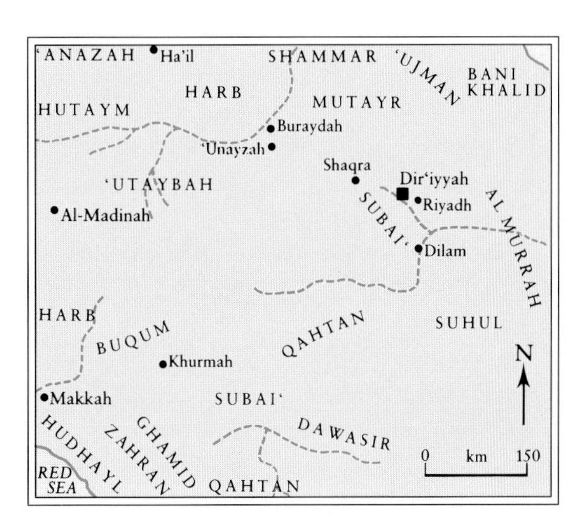

The tribes of Najd

the raw material of everyday life. But other essential items were needed for the year, and in winter and spring it produced a surplus of cheese, clarified butter and livestock, which would be taken to the settlements to be exchanged for them: dates, rice, wheat, coffee, cardamum, weapons, camel equipment, household implements and cash. Secondary items traded by the bedouin were raw wool, woven textiles and tanned hides. The trade in livestock was sometimes conducted by traders who came out from the settlements to the bedouin encampments. Similarly, the settlements depended upon the bedouin for many of their animal products and much of their transport and animal power.

Yet if he made the transition to settled life, the nomad adopted a different set of interests from those of his previous life. These often brought him into conflict with the nomadic tribes. The most frequent bones of contention were grazing and water rights. A strong settlement would always try to extend its area of influence by creating *hima*s or grazing reserves in the vicinity, which might conflict with rights claimed by the bedouin. Equally, and especially in times of drought, a strong nomadic group might seek to deprive a settlement of its wells and to graze on marginal agricultural land.

This conflict of interest was reinforced by the contempt which the true nomad felt for the settler – an attitude which could prevent him from appreciating the extent to which he was dependent upon settlers, and which strengthened his view of himself as a free and autonomous agent. Settlers, on the other hand, were more ambivalent about the bedouin. Since many settled families were themselves of nomadic origin, they shared the view of the essential nobility of nomadic life and the beauties of the desert; but, at the same time, they might despise the *badawi* for his relative poverty and lack of sophistication. In times of conflict, contempt could be mixed with fear of the *badawi*'s tendency to resort to force, although he was also notorious for the fickleness of his loyalties.

Tentative population figures in 19th century sources suggest that settled people outnumbered the nomads in Lower Najd, and this had probably been the case since the 16th and 17th centuries. In any event, the Najdi townsmen were doughty fighters, quite capable of repulsing bedouin raids. Hence the larger towns, if sufficiently well organised, were able to deal with the bedouin tribes on a basis of equality, and even, in favourable times, to dominate them. A town often developed a special relationship with a particular nomadic group, which would then use the town to fulfil whatever needs it had of settlers to the exclusion of other nomads. Villages and smaller settlements, by contrast, were at the mercy of the bedouin, either paying them tribute in the form of wheat, dates and clothes – basically a protection tax – or simply being vulnerable to pillage by them.

Beneath the surface of the nomad-settler conflict, it is clear that neither would have been able to exist without each other. Between them, they enabled both crop-growing and stock-rearing to be realised in an optimal way in a harsh environment. If anything, the nomads were more dependent on the existence of the settlements than vice versa. But it is more useful to view the whole nomad-settler spectrum as a range of possible ways of exploiting the entire environment – ways to which a tribally-organised society could adapt according to changing circumstances. In this way Najdi society maximised its options and, in so doing, its chances of survival.

CHAPTER THREE

In the Beginning

The origins of the Dir‘iyyah settlements

THE FOUNDATION OF DIR‘IYYAH

The foundation of Dir‘iyyah is traditionally ascribed to the year AD 1446. As we have seen, this took place as part of a rapid growth in the population of Lower Najd in the 15th century, when new settlers revived old towns, important new settlements were founded, and new nomadic tribes had been attracted into the region. The two most important towns of Wadi Hanifah, Dir‘iyyah and ‘Uyaynah, both traced their origins to this time.

The tradition of Dir‘iyyah's foundation is preserved by the Najdi chroniclers. The appearance of these chroniclers, from the early 17th century, is itself an indication of the revival of Najdi towns and the literary pursuits which settled life made possible. The chroniclers were concerned to record as much as they could of the history of the settlements and their ruling families, and set down their information as far as possible on a year-by-year basis, in the style of traditional annals.

The story goes that Ibn Dir‘, chief of the Al Dir‘ clan of the Duru‘ of Banu Hanifah, was anxious about the decline of his clan's power and influence in the area. This was probably in response to the re-settlement proceeding elsewhere, and he decided to try to rectify the situation in the time-honoured manner, by inviting new settlers into his domain. As chief of Hajr and Jiz‘ah, he controlled a fertile section of Wadi Hanifah which was not being utilised, and he turned to another Duru‘ clan of Banu Hanifah who at that time were living near Qatif on the Gulf coast, at a place named Dir‘iyyah. This clan, named the Muradah, was attracted by the proposition and, under their leader, Mani‘ al-Muraydi, they made the

move in about 1446. Ibn Dir' gave them the plots of Ghasibah and Mulaybid in the Wadi Hanifah, in the northern part of his lands where they bordered on the territory of the old Banu Hanifah clan of Al Yazid.

The Muradah named their new settlement Dir'iyyah after their old home. The new Dir'iyyah expanded rapidly with this infusion of new blood. Within a few years, under its first three shaykhs, they had deprived Al Yazid of the remainder of their holdings and expelled them. By the beginning of the 16th century, power over all the settlements of the northern Wadi Hanifah was divided between 'Uyaynah and Dir'iyyah with the line at Jubaylah. Dir'iyyah had attracted new settlers, and visitors and traders flocked to it.

So Dir'iyyah became the focus of its part of Wadi Hanifah. In the early 16th century, during the rule of Ibrahim ibn Musa, the fourth chief of Dir'iyyah, the ruling clan, which had greatly expanded, began to segment. One branch left to settle at Durma across the Jabal Tuwayq to the west, where they eventually became the ruling family. Another branch moved to Aba al-Kibash north of Dir'iyyah.

Meanwhile Hajr lost its importance, no doubt as the result of Dir'iyyah's rise, and fragmented into a series of small villages. Hajr is not referred to any longer in the sources under that name. Instead, two of its villages achieved a certain prominence, first Mi'kal in the 16th century, and later Muqrin. In the 17th century the area of Hajr began to be known as Riyadh – the Gardens. Mi'kal and then Muqrin seem to have been at least as important as Dir'iyyah up until the early 18th century. The 17th century Turkish geographer Hajji Khalfa described Muqrin as a town situated near Dir'iyyah with 700 houses constructed of clay. He describes Dir'iyyah itself merely as lying on the route between al-Hasa and Makkah, although it is perhaps significant that he uses it as his central point around which he orientates many other of the Najdi settlements he names.

'Uyaynah, in the northern part of the Wadi Hanifah, developed similarly after its foundation in the 15th century. The ruling clan Al Mu'ammar, of the settled tribe of Tamim, extended its influence over Wadi Qurran, the old Banu Hanifah settlement

The imposing ruins of Turayf, dominated by the Palace of Sa'd (left), show the House of Saud's power in the late 18th and early 19th centuries.

area to the north. Al Mu'ammar were more cohesive than the *ru'asa'* of Dir'iyyah – a factor which was to help them to make 'Uyaynah the pre-eminent town of Najd in the 17th and early 18th centuries. Hajji Khalfa refers to it as a beautiful town north-west of Dir'iyyah and praises its fruits.

By 1600 the population of Lower Najd was probably as high as it had ever been. An indication of the new prosperity is provided by the interest shown in Najd by the Sharifs of Makkah. In fact, the period from 1578 onwards is one of the few in which an outside power has shown more than a passing interest in central Arabia. In 1517 the Ottomans had assumed control of Egypt and the Hijaz and, in so doing, had bolstered the power and authority of the Sharifs. Shortly after, Jabrid power in al-Hasa declined in the face of Portuguese incursions into the Gulf. The Ottomans, anxious to counter both Persian power and the Portuguese threat to trade in the Indian Ocean after 1498, extended their dominion into southern Iraq and thence into eastern Arabia. In about 1550 they took over al-Hasa Oasis, making their provincial capital at Hofuf, known to them as Lahsa.

With the Ottomans in control of western and eastern Arabia, the Sharifs of Makkah felt in a strong position to enlarge their sphere of influence into newly prosperous Najd. The first recorded attack took place in 1578 and was directed against the settlement of Mi'kal. The son of the incumbent Sharif Abu Numay II is said to have descended upon the town with no fewer than 50,000 troops, killing many, plundering the place, taking hostages and installing a governor. He forced the chiefs of Mi'kal and its surrounding area, presumably including Dir'iyyah to submit and hand over large amounts of local produce. Three years later he campaigned into al-Kharj.

This stone-built wall, seen here in section, protected the early town of Ghasibah.

In all, eighteen Sharifian invasions of Najd are recorded up until the early 18th century. Notable was one in 1647 when the Sharif Zaid ibn Muhsin forced 'Uyaynah to hand over a large amount of money and three hundred camel-loads of produce. The expeditions were directed as much against the nomads as the settlements. Although they seem on the face of it to have tried to impose some kind of political control on the region, by taking hostages and installing sympathetic chiefs, such gains were always shortlived and fell far short of the establishment of lasting central authority. Guarantees of good behaviour by the tribes, especially in abstaining from molesting the pilgrimages, and the exaction of tribute were the prime results. But the tribute was never paid regularly and its collection required renewed campaigning.

The expeditions seem to have been chiefly motivated by a need to bring food supplies to Makkah, as the expeditions into Najd returned with great caravans of dates and wheat. The productive and populous farming settlements of Lower Najd had clearly developed into tempting targets since their foundation in the 15th century.

DIR'IYYAH AND 'UYAYNAH, 1600-1725

Between 1620 and 1676 six droughts are recorded, while only four are recorded for the entire previous period since 1446. These droughts placed a new stress on the Najdi population. In that period many of the nomads and settlers were forced to migrate away from Najd towards the east and north, while other nomads abandoned their precarious existence to settle. Meanwhile various other nomadic tribes were arriving in Najd in the late 16th and 17th centuries: Zafir, 'Anazah and Dawasir, followed by Mutayr, Banu Khalid and Qahtan. After 1676 conditions improved somewhat, there being only three droughts recorded up to 1738. But in this latter period the recording of disastrous events becomes more detailed, and we are made aware of the other scourges: disease and locust attack. Both could cripple settlements without warning.

As a result of the droughts in the 17th century, many of Dir'iyyah's people, with others from Lower Najd, migrated to Zubayr at the head of the Gulf south-west of Basra. Great influxes of Najdis were drawn there, partly by its trading potential, particularly after the great drought of AD 1637-8. Zubayr very quickly became a predominantly Najdi town, important in the caravan trade.

The complicated tale of the feuding within the Muradah clan for the leadership of Dir'iyyah perfectly illustrates political conditions within the average Najdi settlement before the reform movement. Divisions within the Muradah continued until, by the middle of the 17th century, two main groups emerged as rivals for the

Ghasibah *(above and left)* **has lain in ruins since its capture by Ibrahim Pasha's trooops in 1818. With Mulaybid, it is said to have been Dir'iyyah's earliest settlement, pre-dating Turayf, by which it was supplanted probably in the 17th century. Its stout fortification wall** *(right)* **survives on its northern side.**

chieftainship: Al Muqrin and Al Watban (also known as Al Rabi'ah). The sources suggest that this rivalry was reflected in the plan of the town which, as so often in Najd, was divided into two quarters, Dir'iyyah itself – by this probably Turayf is meant – and Ghasibah, on opposite sides of Wadi Hanifah. As we have seen, Ghasibah was one of the original settlements of the Muradah in 1446, and so is thought to be the oldest quarter of Dir'iyyah. In 1654 Rabi'ah's son Watban acquired the amirate of Ghasibah by murdering his cousin, Markhan ibn Muqrin, who had usurped him in the chieftainship. This suggests that Ghasibah was at that time, if not the chief settlement of Dir'iyyah, then at least a rival to Turayf in importance, reflecting the rivalry of the two clans. Today it is an extensive ruin field, testifying like the ruins of Turayf to its destruction and abandonment after 1819.

Until the early 18th century most of the rulers of Dir'iyyah came from Al Watban, although in the immediate aftermath of Watban's recovery of Ghasibah in 1654, the Muqrin branch regained the rulership, in the person of Muhammad ibn Muqrin. Muhammad's son Nasir was amir of Dir'iyyah in 1673, and another son, Saud, the founder of the present ruling family, was later to re-assert Al Muqrin's claim.

Despite the environmental uncertainty and the strife among its *ru'asa'*, Dir'iyyah enjoyed a moderate prosperity throughout this period. Except in times of drought or locust attack, both Dir'iyyah and Durma were noted for their agricultural production and low prices. But Dir'iyyah does not seem to have achieved more prominence than the average Najdi settlement, and the recording of the details of its ruling family was inspired by what came later. Throughout the period up to 1725 'Uyaynah outshone Dir'iyyah in size, commerce, strength and political prestige.

In 1670 the Banu Khalid tribe of al-Hasa ejected the Ottomans and took control of the two great oases of al-Hasa and Qatif. Being a bedouin tribe they also maintained effective control of the desert, unlike their Turkish predecessors. After 1670 the Banu Khalid took an increasing interest in Najd. Their expeditions were directed chiefly against nomadic tribes, probably in order to make the trade routes safe. But they also fostered relations with the Najdi settlements, again because of commercial relations. They did not interfere in the towns' internal affairs by installing governors or even it seems by imposing any regular taxation. They did however exercise an influence over them, particularly at 'Uyaynah, the principal town of southern Najd at this time. Only in the case of Dir'iyyah does it seem that the Banu Khalid had any direct involvement: for it appears that they raided it in 1682, and then from 1694 until 1709, two rulers who may have been of Banu Khalid origin installed themselves there. In 1709 the second one was assassinated and replaced by a member of the Watban clan, Musa ibn Rabi'ah ibn Watban.

The Banu Khalid leader Sa'dun ibn Muhammad, who ruled al-Hasa firmly from 1691 till 1723, took a close interest in Najd and campaigned there frequently, in alliance with 'Uyaynah. In 1721 this alliance turned against Dir'iyyah when Sa'dun besieged and bombarded 'Aqraba and 'Ammariyyah, and then turned on Dir'iyyah. He plundered its gardens and destroyed many houses in the villages of Zuhayrah, Surayhah and Malwi, but the people defended themselves and Sa'dun withdrew.

The Banu Khalid choice of 'Uyaynah as its ally in Lower Najd was a sound one. By the middle of the 17th century, 'Uyaynah had become the most expansionist town in southern Najd. Under its ruling clan Al Mu'ammar, its influence extended northwards to include Huraymila and Malham. Unlike the Muradah of Dir'iyyah, Al Mu'ammar was cohesive and 'Uyaynah was largely free of internal strife.

From 1659 till 1725 AD the town had just two rulers. The later of them, Abdullah ibn Muhammad Ibn Mu'ammar, expanded his influence northwards to Thadiq. By his reign 'Uyaynah was already a great commercial centre, importing piece-goods from the Hasa coast. In a feud with Huraymila he allied himself with Dir'iyyah but, in the 1680s, he turned his attention southwards and so encroached on the sphere of his southern neighbour. Thereafter Dir'iyyah, Huraymila and al-Kharj made common cause against him. But 'Uyaynah remained the strongest town in southern Najd. In the early 18th century its alliance with the Banu Khalid greatly strengthened its hand in raids on Dir'iyyah and al-Kharj.

By the early 18th century 'Uyaynah's buildings and agricultural development were the wonder of central Arabia. It had become the strongest regional authority that Najd had produced since Hajr in the Early Islamic period, and we are lucky to have an eye-witness report of it during its heyday. In 1709 a Damascene traveller, Murtada ibn Ali ibn 'Alawan, made the pilgrimage to Makkah. He returned through Najd on his way to Baghdad via Tharmida and 'Uyaynah. Unfortunately he did not visit Dir'iyyah but what he has to say about 'Uyaynah is of some interest. He praises its citrus fruit and "such precious things as are only to be found in Damascus". Its water, all of course drawn from wells, was unusually pure, and its people had very many means of gaining a livelihood. He does not say what these were, but the inference must be that there was a diversity of trades which singled 'Uyaynah out from other Arabian towns that he visited. The civilised Murtada left 'Uyaynah much refreshed after his month-long journey from the Hijaz, and continued his way to al-Hasa, where he praises the harmonious rule of Sa'dun.

At some time before 1720 Saud ibn Muhammad of the Muqrin branch assumed the chieftainship of Dir'iyyah from Musa ibn Rabi'ah and, in so doing, became the eponymous founder of the House of Saud. Saud ibn Muhammad ruled until his death in 1725 and was succeeded by a member of Al Watban, Zaid ibn Markhan. This episode exemplified the difficulties of smooth succession within the divided *ru'asa'* of a Najdi town, for Saud's brother Muqrin, while professing loyalty to the new ruler, privately thought himself entitled to rule. Muqrin invited Zaid to a meeting to confirm their understanding of his loyalty. Zaid, who was suspicious, agreed on condition that two relatives of Muqrin be present to guarantee his safety. One of these relatives was the son of Saud and future ruler, Muhammad ibn Saud.

During the meeting it became clear that Muqrin intended treachery on his guest, and the two relatives, true to their pledge, threw themselves on him and, after a brief chase in which Muqrin escaped through a window and hid, killed him. We can see here that Muhammad ibn Saud had already gained the reputation for honouring pledges which was to become a hallmark of Dir'iyyah's Imams in later decades.

Zaid's rule was brief. He was killed in the following year in an abortive expedition against 'Uyaynah. In 1725-6, 'Uyaynah was in the throes of a local epidemic which carried off most of its population including Abdullah ibn Muhammad, by then the most respected ruler in all Najd. It was in a weak position, and Zaid of Dir'iyyah took his opportunity to move against it. Leading a force in company with Muhammad ibn Saud, he occupied 'Aqraba, where 'Uyaynah's new ruler Kharfash proposed a meeting to negotiate. Zaid agreed, and Kharfash's men killed him as he took his seat in the reception room. Muhammad ibn Saud managed to negotiate a pledge of safety for himself and his men, and retired to Dir'iyyah. Muhammad ibn Saud then assumed the rulership and expelled Al Watban from Dir'iyyah.

Al Watban went to Zubayr, where they joined their relatives, and eventually became the ruling family there. Muhammad ibn Saud ruled until his death in 1765 - a momentous reign, during which Dir'iyyah became the centre of the reform movement. But the start of his rule was marked by 'Uyaynah's recovery from its epidemic, and its resumption of its former dominance of Najdi affairs. Together with another Tamim town, Ushayqir in al-Washm, it was the most important centre of learning and Shari'ah law in Najd. It had been known for its *'ulama'* since the 16th century, and contact with the Hanbali centre of learning in Damascus was strong. During the 17th and early 18th century the number and influence of its teachers and men of the law increased. As the birthplace of Shaykh Muhammad ibn 'Abd al-Wahhab, it was his natural first choice as the centre from which to propagate his reform movement, to which we shall turn in the next chapter.

Husayn ibn Ghannam, the chronicler of the reform movement who died in 1810, takes a very dim view of the laxity of religious observance among the people of Najd before the appearance on the scene of Shaykh Muhammad ibn 'Abd al-Wahhab in the early 18th century. But it is evident from the increase of *'ulama'* in the Najdi towns, especially from the 17th century, that intellectual opposition was growing to what was perceived as backsliding from the true faith. In view of this, it is interesting that Dir'iyyah is recorded as having had a Shari'ah judge in the 17th century. In addition, at least two pilgrimages are recorded by notables from Dir'iyyah in the 17th century. One was in 1630, when Ibrahim ibn Musa's grandson, Rabi'ah, himself chief of Dir'iyyah, and his brother Muqrin, visited Makkah during the year of the great flood which almost destroyed the Ka'bah. Another was in 1680, when various notables arrived from Dir'iyyah to perform the *haj* and visit the Sharif.

CHAPTER FOUR

An Idea is Born

Muhammad ibn 'Abd al-Wahhab is heard

THE BIRTH OF THE REFORM MOVEMENT

As settlement increased and settled values took hold, a growing concern with learning and the principles of good government according to Islamic precepts took root in Najd. The numbers of *'ulama'*, or scholars versed in Islamic law, rose century by century. Fifteen are recorded for the 16th century. Ushayqir, the old Tamim town in al-Washm, emerges as the chief centre of learning, with no fewer than nine of them, followed by Muqrin with two and 'Uyaynah, among other towns, with one. Five of them visited Damascus or Cairo to study under leading scholars of the Hanbali school of Islamic law.

In the 17th century the recorded figure for *'ulama'* rose to twenty-eight, including fifteen from Ushayqir and six from 'Uyaynah. Several of these scholars moved to other towns in Najd to serve as *qadi*s or judges – including the first recorded one to Dir'iyyah. Others taught and preached in their towns, so fuelling the spread of religious awareness and learning among the townsfolk. By the 18th century Najd and al-Hasa had become, with Damascus and Cairo, important centres for Hanbali studies.

The great reformer Shaykh Muhammad ibn 'Abd al Wahhab conceived his mission in this climate of rising intellectual and religious activity among the townspeople of Najd. Under the impact of his reform movement the 18th century saw an even greater rise in the number of *'ulama'*, whose influence was enhanced still further by their spread to even more towns. No fewer than fifty-two are recorded. As settlements grew in population and complexity, the learned scholars of the law were needed to fulfil a number of functions: as *imam*s (prayer leaders), *qadi*s (judges of Islamic law), and *mufti*s (legal advisers, particularly to the rulers). They provided a much needed service in settling disputes, as the emphasis on law and the production of legal manuals shows.

In some of the settlements, until the first half of the 18th century, the *'ulama'* were opposed and even ejected by the rulers, because they found their rulings inconvenient – as was to happen to the Shaykh himself at 'Uyaynah. But, by the last third of the 18th century and the establishment of the First Saudi State on the principles propounded by the Shaykh, the triumph of Islamic law in Najd was to be complete. The career of the Shaykh marked the point at which the *'ulama'* achieved equal status and power in government with the rulers themselves – a relationship which was to be embodied for the first time in the mode of government at Dir'iyyah.

The increase in learning in the Najdi towns had effects beyond the study of Islamic law. Some *'ulama'* began to write histories. Composed in the form of year-by-year chronicles, these records of events survive almost entirely from the 18th century and after, though one has come down to us from the 17th. The most important are by Husayn ibn Ghannam and 'Uthman ibn Bishr.

As one would expect, both Ibn Ghannam and Ibn Bishr were fervent supporters of the reform movement. Ibn Ghannam's *Rawdat al- Afkar* chronicles the life and works of Shaykh Muhammad ibn 'Abd al Wahhab. Ibn Ghannam's death in 1810 coincided with the apogee of Dir'iyyah's power, and so his life was contemporary with many of the events about which he wrote. Ibn Bishr's work *'Unwan al-Majd fi Ta'rikh Najd* is the most comprehensive primary source on the history of the reform movement. He condenses Ibn Ghannam's work on the early period and brings the story up to 1853. He lived from 1795 until 1873, and so his adult life coincided with the end of the First Saudi State

The Mosque of Shaykh Muhammad ibn 'Abd al-Wahhab in Bujayri is carefully preserved. Directly across the Wadi Hanifah from Turayf, Bujayri was the centre of the Shaykh's reforming mission. Here he came to live with his large family and followers after his reception at Dir'iyyah in 1745.

and the best part of the Second Saudi State. Besides giving a bald record of events, both Ibn Ghannam and Ibn Bishr provide insights into conditions of life in Najd both before and during their time.

Hence it is from Ibn Ghannam that we have an early account of religious practices amongst the general populace of Najd before the reform movement. From what he describes it is evident that there was considerable laxity in the observance of Islamic precepts, and that various pagan superstitions had either taken hold or had

The restored wall of Turayf and Faisal Tower *(above)*, looking much as Shaykh Muhammad ibn ʻAbd al-Wahhab might have seen them, are reflected in flood water in the bed of the Wadi Hanifah.

persisted since the pre-Islamic period. People used to hold sacred the tombs of some of the Companions of the Prophet who fell at the Battle of ʻAqraba near Jubaylah in AD 634, including that of Zaid ibn al-Khattab, the brother of the second Caliph ʻUmar. Certain trees were visited as part of a fertility cult, and a cave was venerated. A "holy man" from al-Kharj was revered by his followers as a miracle-worker with the power to fulfil their wishes. He was alleged to be blind but to need no guide, and commanded allegiance among the people and rulers of Dirʻiyyah and neighbouring towns.

Such accretions typified the contemporary Islamic world and Najd was not unusual in this respect. Despite these practices the townspeople of Najd were still good Muslims by the standards of their time, in that they prayed and attended their mosques. As we have seen, many of them made the pilgrimage. It was the reformist historians' own view that such practices disqualified their adherents from being considered as Muslims. The contemporary Muslim world at large held a different view. Yet the Najdi townsfolk and some of their rulers were becoming more and more receptive to the new thinking, and the clarion call of the Shaykh, which reverberates through Arabian history right up to the present day, was to find ready listeners.

Shaykh Muhammad ibn ʻAbd al Wahhab was born in 1703 in ʻUyaynah. He came of the scholarly Tamim tribe of Wuhabah of Ushayqir in al-Washm, and so was very much the product of the two chief centres of learning in Najd during the previous century and more. His grandfather had been *qadi* and *mufti* of ʻUyaynah, while his father ʻAbd al-Wahhab was one of the most distinguished *ʻulama'* of his time, serving as *qadi* of ʻUyaynah from 1713 till 1726-7. He left ʻUyaynah after a disagreement with its ruler, Kharfash, and moved to Huraymila where he also became *qadi*.

The young Muhammad's father recognised his son's precocious talent for his studies. "I have often," he is reported as having said, "in forming my decisions, been benefited by the opinions of my son Muhammad." In about 1723 Muhammad left ʻUyaynah to further his studies in Makkah, Madinah and then Basra. He had also intended to study in Damascus, the centre of Hanbali studies which had attracted many previous Najdi *ʻulama'*. But his preaching against the cult of holy men and his growing influence caused him to be expelled. By now he was penniless, and he abandoned all thoughts of going to Damascus. He left Basra, on foot, and travelled via Zubayr to al-Hasa, where he continued his studies. From there he re-joined his father, who was by now at Huraymila, staying with him until his death in 1740.

From then on he began to propagate his views zealously in Huraymila, once again provoking opposition from the established *ʻulama'*. During this time he publicised his ideas of reform in his famous work, *Kitab al-Tawhid, The Book of the Oneness of God*,

and strongly denounced the superstitions prevailing in Najd, appealing to those in authority to support him. He decided to seek the protection of the ruler of 'Uyaynah, 'Uthman ibn Hamad Al Mu'ammar. He was welcomed, and the ruler and many of the people were converted to the new movement, which immediately began to cleanse 'Uyaynah of improper practices and places of veneration. Sacred trees were uprooted, and domes over tombs such as that of Zaid ibn al-Khattab were demolished, to the chagrin of the people of Jubaylah. A woman who had confessed to adultery was stoned to death.

However, news of the Shaykh's doings was brought to the ears of the Banu Khalid ruler of al-Hasa, Sulayman ibn Muhammad ibn Ghurayr, by whose consent 'Uthman Ibn Mu'ammar ruled 'Uyaynah. Sulayman threatened to withdraw the subsidy which he paid to 'Uyaynah unless the new movement was stopped. 'Uthman had been a loyal friend to the Shaykh, and sincere in the commendation of virtue and condemnation of vice in 'Uyaynah, but he owed his position to the Banu Khalid leader and this was a sacrifice which he felt unable to make. With great reluctance he requested Shaykh Muhammad to leave. And the Shaykh did so, choosing Dir'iyyah as his next destination.

'Uthman Ibn Mu'ammar furnished him with an escort of horsemen, the Shaykh himself going on foot, with no more than a fan to ward off the afternoon heat. The escort abandoned the Shaykh by a cave on the way – which was the tomb of a saintly *darwish* – leaving him to trudge on alone. As he did so, he must have reflected, not for the first time, on the lot of prophets who are without honour in their own country.

Top: **Shaykh Muhammad ibn 'Abd al-Wahhab was to make his home in Bujayri, which nestled among the palms seen here below the wall on the heights of Jabal Qurayn, with Turayf in the background.**

Above: **Flood waters swirl beneath the ruins of Turayf.**

Eventually he reached the northern end of the oasis of Dir'iyyah, and called at the house of Muhammad ibn Suwaylim al-'Urayni. Ibn Suwaylim was frightened that the Amir of Dir'iyyah, Muhammad ibn Saud, would find out, but agreed to extend his hospitality to the Shaykh. Awareness of the Shaykh's presence and its significance began to spread among some of the notables of Dir'iyyah, and people came to visit him to hear his teaching. These people, including some of the Amir's brothers, wanted to promote the Shaykh's cause with Muhammad ibn Saud, and considered how best to do so.

The plan they hit on was to tell his wife, Mudi bint Abu Watban. Mudi was known to be a wise woman who might be sympathetic to the Shaykh' s message, and so it turned out. She persuaded her husband that God had placed a treasure at his disposal which he would be foolish to ignore. Muhammad ibn Saud was persuaded to investigate. It was even arranged that he should go up the Wadi on foot to Ibn Suwaylim's house, as a public mark of honour to persuade others to visit the Shaykh and to forestall persecution.

It was to be an historic encounter. Shaykh Muhammad ibn 'Abd al Wahhab explained to Muhammad ibn Saud that, by going back to the original principles of Islam, he would be assured of strength and wealth in this world and in the hereafter. The Shaykh was evidently possessed of a charismatic presence, as we are told that "God cast into the heart of Muhammad ibn Saud the love of the Shaykh." Muhammad ibn Saud bade the Shaykh "Welcome to a country better than your country: you shall have all honour and support from us."

But, practical man that he was, he sought assurances from the Shaykh on two points. The first was that the Shaykh should not leave Dir'iyyah to go elsewhere after their joint mission had begun. The second showed the typical anxiety of the traditional Najdi ruler when faced with the possibility of having his tax base replaced by *zakah*.

He said, "I am entitled by the laws of my land to certain revenues on the earnings of my subjects from agriculture and trade and the rest. You will not ask me to forgo this right." The Shaykh replied: "As for the first matter, give me your hand on it. And as for the second, Almighty God will bring you conquests and recompense you with spoils of war far more ample than your present revenues."

Muhammad ibn Saud was convinced, and thus was born the religio-political pact between the Shaykh and the ruler of Dir'iyyah. Muhammad ibn Saud agreed to support the doctrines of the Shaykh politically and militarily, in exchange for the Shaykh's assurance of support and advice. The year was 1745. It marks the beginning of the rise to power of the First Saudi State, and the partnership between ruler and religious mentor which characterised it.

The central thrust of Shaykh Muhammad's reform movement was a return to the primal strictness of early Islam, a rejection of religious innovation and a restriction of interpretation. He followed the teachings of Ibn Hanbal, the 9th century founder of the most conservative of the four orthodox Sunni schools of Islamic law.

Ibn Hanbal's teachings were approached through the work of the Syrian Hanbali Ibn

Above: **Flood waters tumble down the cliff into the gardens just west of Turayf on the day after a storm. Such floods were allowed to flow through culverts under Dir'iyyah's wall, with such force that they might sometimes demolish a section of it.**

Left: **The southern defence tower of Turayf, seen from the farm beneath, has been restored.**

Left: **The walls and towers protecting Dir'iyyah were built along the top of the limestone cliffs on each side of Wadi Hanifah. This layered limestone was a convenient source of building material.**

Taymiyyah (1262-1328 AD), the theologian and jurist who advocated unswerving adherence to the Qur'an and Sunnah, or Tradition of the Prophet, and condemned saint worship, the veneration of shrines and other innovations. Ibn Taymiyyah vigorously opposed the popular "innovations" associated with Sufism, and called for a return to pristine Islam in law and practice. As was to happen to his intellectual heir Shaykh Muhammad ibn 'Abd al Wahhab, his teaching made him unpopular with the rulers of his time and angered the *'ulama'*. Ibn Taymiyyah was persecuted and died in prison.

The fundamental dogma of the movement was *tawhid*, the Oneness or Unity of God – hence the name *muwahhidun* by which the Shaykh and his followers liked to be known. Nothing can be compared to God, or draw near to Him, or be associated with Him. Hence the attempt to worship Him through the intercession of saints or Companions of the Prophet (*shirk*, or association) was considered a heresy tantamount to polytheism, meriting death. This was at the root of their puritan zeal in the destruction of shrines and tombs, and their justification for *jihad*, or holy war, in spreading their doctrines among the heretics.

The community of believers' whole purpose was to apply God's law, before which all men are equal. The ruler's responsibility was to ensure that the Shari'ah was rigorously applied, and to spread the rule of God's law to all men – hence the martial face of reform and the constant state of *jihad* or holy war in its early days. The ruler's actions should be undertaken with the counsel of religious advisers – the *'ulama'* – and enforced by a sort of religious police – the *mutawwi's* or "obedience causers". In such a community, there could be no perceived distinction between religious and secular matters. Dir'iyyah was the crucible in which the attempt was made to give political and social expression to these religious tenets.

In the Shaykh's view, the use of saints to intercede with God put its practitioners beyond the pale of Islam. That is why he and his followers referred to themselves simply as Muslims, thus distancing themselves from what they regarded as the heresies of the Islamic world around them. The other term for them, *muwahhidun* or "Unitarians", was less frequently used. Although they are known to outsiders as Wahhabis, after the founder of the movement, that term was one coined originally by the movement's detractors – though it has long since lost any derogatory connotation, and its widespread use makes it a convenient term to use.

CHAPTER FIVE

Al Saud Ascendant

The reformist state expands

DIR'IYYAH EXTENDS ITS AUTHORITY IN NAJD, 1745-1785

With the pact in 1745 between Shaykh Muhammad ibn 'Abd al-Wahhab and Muhammad ibn Saud, Dir'iyyah became the centre of the militant reforming mission which was to change the course of Arabian history. It says much for the power of the Shaykh's personality that, until his death in 1792 almost half a century later, he was effectively co-regent of Dir'iyyah and its growing empire in Arabia.

The doctrines of the new movement were recognised by contemporary European observers such as Niebuhr, Brydges, Ali Bey and Burckhardt as no more than the fundamental principles of Islam. It was the way in which the new movement chose to spread its message which understandably gave rise to alarm and misunderstanding. *Jihad*, or holy war, with its insistence on killing those who were regarded as heretical and decadent Muslim opponents, was not a way to attract a sympathetic following. As a result, the Ottomans and Egyptians consistently sought to portray it in their propaganda as not only dangerous but heretical. It is true that Wahhabi divines were often keen to counter the charge of heresy by argument, to demonstrate the purity of their beliefs, when they were in the Holy Cities or farther afield, for example in al-Azhar University in Cairo. *Jihad* was, however, an effective way to combine proselytism with plunder, which made it attractive to the tribesmen and brought revenue to the state. This helps at once to explain the success of the movement and its ultimate failure to take hold beyond the borders of Najd.

Despite the purity of its doctrines, the reform movement in its early days made slow progress. While winning adherents among the people of many towns in Lower Najd, it faced opposition from their rulers. To begin with the forces at Dir'iyyah's disposal were far from threatening, sometimes numbering, it is said, just a few camel-riders. But this time the threat was not simply that posed by traditional power-seeking, or by one clan seeking to oust another – although this was a factor. The threat lay also in the new ideology, which sought to establish a central authority under the rule of Shari'ah law. In doing so, local rivalries were to be suppressed, and customary law and taxation practices overridden. As the story of Muhammad ibn Saud's first meeting with the Shaykh illustrates, the loss of his traditional tax base was often uppermost in a ruler's mind.

Until the flight of its ruler Diham ibn Dawwas in 1773, Riyadh was the focus of resistance in Najd to Dir'iyyah's mission. The chroniclers record some thirty-five clashes between the two towns during the period 1746-1773. The loss of life was considerable – said to have been altogether about 4000 men, of whom 1700 were from Dir'iyyah and 2300 from Riyadh. Eliminating the threat from Riyadh was a significant step: Dir'iyyah could turn its attention to the rest of Najd.

Raiding parties from Dir'iyyah and its allies attacked Riyadh almost annually until 1758. Such forays were usually small-scale skirmishes, relying on surprise and leaving few dead. At the same time Dir'iyyah was faced with problems in maintaining its alliances, as hostile factions within allied towns might occasionally seize the initiative and declare against it. 'Abd al-'Aziz ibn Muhammad, son of the Saudi ruler, had been since 1750 the Unitarians' usual commander in battle, and by 1753-4 Diham had grown tired of the constant threat from his neighbour and entered into a truce. As was customary on these occasions, Dir'iyyah sent a learned shaykh of reform to instruct his people.

The truce lasted about a year before Diham was emboldened to oppose Dir'iyyah once more. Opposition to the reform movement had clearly grown by this time in a number of Najdi towns, as this time Riyadh was supported by Manfuhah, Tharmida, and elements from Thadiq, Huraymila and towns in al-Washm and Sudayr. As under all such régimes, the subjects could be divided into those who resented the harsh disciplines of the reformers, and those who regarded the privations as a worthwhile price to pay in establishing the community of believers.

In 1758 the Banu Khalid leader from al-Hasa, 'Uray'ir ibn Dujayn, joined Riyadh and some of the people of al-Kharj and al-Washm in planning an assault from Jubaylah on Dir'iyyah. In the event nothing was gained: the Saudis, as we may now call the supporters of the House of Saud, quickly strengthened the fortifications of Dir'iyyah and other towns. Jubaylah held out and the Banu Khalid withdrew. But from this point until his death in 1774 'Uray'ir posed a constant threat to the reform movement.

The Banu Khalid reverse at Jubaylah boosted the fortunes of Al Saud. Many of the towns renewed their allegiance to Dir'iyyah or submitted to force of arms. In 1762-3 'Abd al-'Aziz defeated the people of Riyadh three times. Later that year he raided a large caravan from al-Hasa bringing goods from the coast, and expropriated the property of the Riyadh merchants. Probably as a

The Mosque of Shaykh Muhammad ibn 'Abd al-Wahhab ***(below and above right)*** **in Bujayri still stands today, a monument to the pact between him and Muhammad ibn Saud, Amir of Dir'iyyah.**

consequence of these reverses, Diham later in the year once again sought a truce.

In the spring of 1764, Dir'iyyah inflicted a defeat on the nomadic 'Ujman tribe. The 'Ujman appealed to their distant kinsmen of Yam, in the Najran region. In a dramatic response, the powerful Makrami lord of Najran, Hasan ibn Hibatullah, anxious about the new religious and political developments in Najd, marched on Wadi Hanifah with a large force. Encamping in the autumn of 1764 at Ha'ir, south of Riyadh, he routed the army of Dir'iyyah and its allies – who for once included Riyadh – which had come out to confront him. Some five hundred men are said to have been killed. After reaching terms the Najrani army quickly withdrew, without following up its advantage. This was fortunate for Dir'iyyah: the Banu Khalid chief 'Uray'ir had arranged to come up from al-Hasa in support of Hasan ibn Hibatullah but, in the event, arrived too late. A desultory three-week campaign in the neighbourhood of Dir'iyyah ensued. The Hasawis, now joined by the people of Riyadh and Manfuhah, deployed cannon against the town with little effect before withdrawing. Evidently Dir'iyyah was well fortified by this time.

In 1765 Muhammad ibn Saud died and was succeeded by his son 'Abd al-'Aziz. Riyadh, having repudiated its truce with Dir'iyyah, once again attacked Manfuhah, this time in concert with the ruler of Dilam and al-Kharj. Over the next three years, 'Abd al-'Aziz mounted unsuccessful assaults on Riyadh. In 1771-2 more concentrated assaults followed, leading in 1773 to Diham's momentous decision to abandon Riyadh for good. Dir'iyyah took possession of all the lands and property left by the fleeing inhabitants, and Riyadh finally lost its independence.

Riyadh's submission removed a persistent opponent, leaving Dir'iyyah free to turn its energies elsewhere. Dir'iyyah's growth as a regional power continued the trend in Najd already set by 'Uyaynah in the late 17th and early 18th centuries. It could count on the support of most towns in Lower Najd, including 'Uyaynah, Manfuhah and the towns in al-Washm, Sudayr and al-Qasim. Raids up to the Euphrates tribes extended its influence further still. But the support was always precarious, and could suddenly disappear within a town if the opposing faction seized the initiative. Hence much of the following decade was spent in restoring the authority of Al Saud where it had lapsed in the towns of Sudayr and al-Qasim.

The rising power of the Saudi state led to the third attempt by the Banu Khalid of al-Hasa, under 'Uray'ir, to destroy it. He invaded al-Qasim in 1774, taking Buraydah, but died shortly thereafter on the way south. The threat evaporated. However, in the following year, a southern Najdi coalition of the people of al-Kharj and Wadi al-Dawasir with the Najran tribes again came against Dir'iyyah. The failure of both expeditions raised Dir'iyyah s prestige, but the towns of al-Kharj continued to resist the Wahhabi cause vigorously until 1785, when they submitted. Wadi al-Dawasir soon followed.

THE ASCENDANCY OF DIR'IYYAH IN ARABIA, 1785-1811

By the late 1780s Dir'iyyah had consolidated its position in Najd to the point where it could turn outwards with confidence. Such confidence had been long in coming – some forty years. From now on events began to flow steadily in its favour. With unity in Najd, larger armies could be levied and the tax base expanded. Raiding parties from Najd had a speed, ferocity and sense of mission which made them feared by their neighbours. The Imam 'Abd al-'Aziz and his son Saud, later to be Saud the Great, were gifted leaders of men and generals in the field.

Ibn Bishr gives us a portrait of the Imam 'Abd al-'Aziz, who emerges as the ideal of the Wahhabi ruler. Until the death of Shaykh Muhammad ibn 'Abd al Wahhab in 1792, no decisions were made without first consulting him, and we get the impression that in terms of ideal Wahhabi governance this period marks the zenith of the reformist state. The Imam 'Abd al-'Aziz himself was devoid of pomp and personal grandeur. He used to sit on the ground, saying "One must be humble as dignity is for God alone." He was not at all extravagant in his manner of dress, nor did his weapons glitter with decoration. He wore only woollen clothes, and his wives wore black without any gold jewelry. His diet was very simple and he ate off wooden plates and drank from a wooden cup. Ibn Bishr compares him favourably with his sons and grandsons, whose swords were decorated with gold and silver, of which 'Abd al-'Aziz himself possessed very little. The Imam was extremely devout, staying in the mosque to pray from the dawn until the midday prayer. Qur'an studies were given priority, and literacy rewarded with prizes for good hand-writing – always a valued accomplishment in Muslim society. His historical knowledge was extensive and he was an entertaining story-teller.

Justice and public order flourished under him. It was said that people could leave their camels and sheep grazing without anybody to tend them, and pilgrims could cross Najd quite unmolested, as theft and banditry had been completely eradicated. If anybody found a stray camel he would bring it to Dir'iyyah to wait for the owner to collect it. Given the usual nature of tribal society, what we have here amounts to a complete revolution in people's values and behaviour.

Meanwhile in al-Hasa 'Uray'ir had been succeeded by his son Sa'dun. Sa'dun ruled firmly for twelve years, and offered his support to Najdi towns wishing to throw off Dir'iyyah's rule. Despite this, the Saudi hold over Najd was sufficiently firm to enable 'Abd al-'Aziz to try to undermine Sa'dun's position in al-Hasa by bribing his opponents in his own tribe. This policy was successful. In 1785 Sa'dun came to Dir'iyyah seeking the

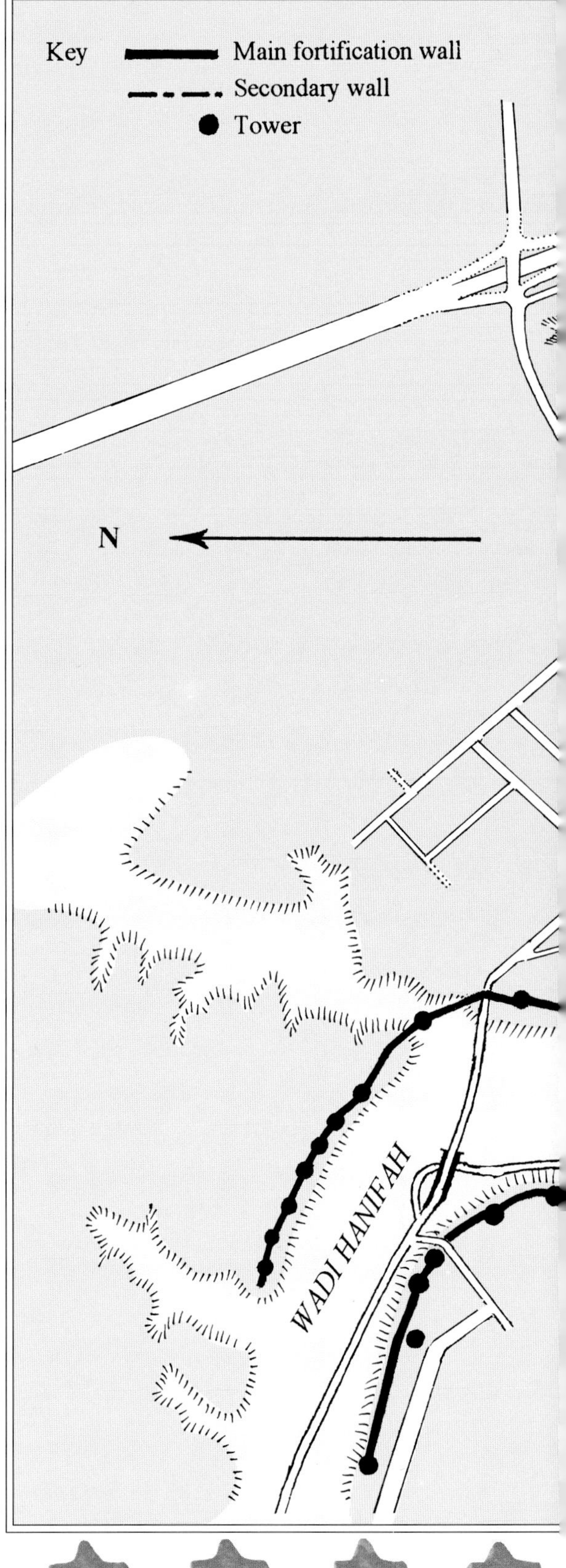

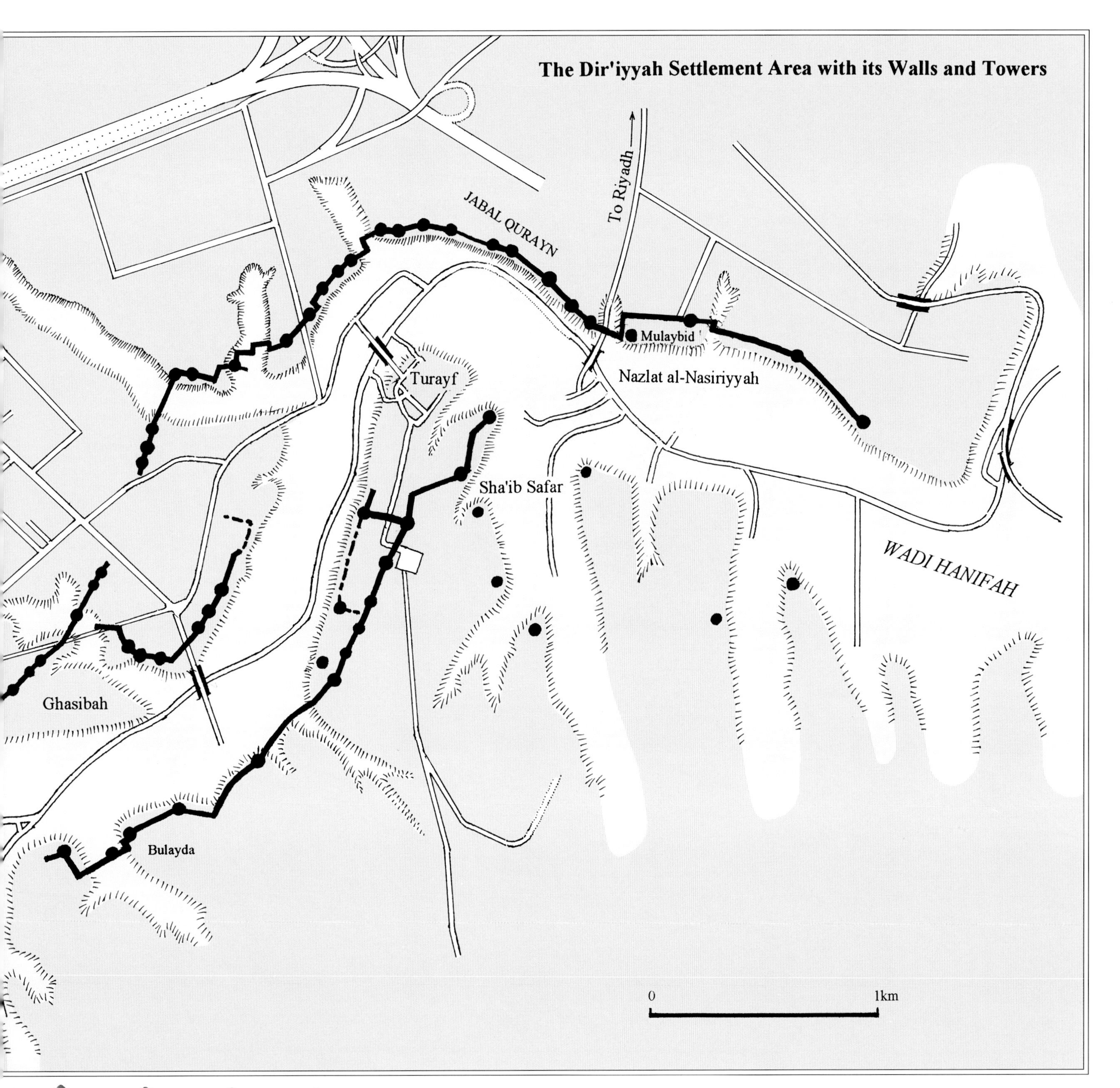

protection of Al Saud against his enemies in al-Hasa. The Imam 'Abd al-'Aziz bided his time, meanwhile sending raiding parties into the Eastern Province. Sa'dun died at Dir'iyyah in 1786. Between 1785 and 1793 Saudi raids on al-Hasa and the Banu Khalid's allies the Muntafiq intensified: in 1788 Saud ibn 'Abd al-'Aziz annihilated the Muntafiq on the Kuwait border, and in 1792 he defeated the Bani Khalid in the same place. By 1795 the submission of al-Hasa was complete. A governor was installed and *'ulama'* and tax-collectors sent in. Raids were mounted into Qatar and against Kuwait, which the *muwahhidun* seem to have harrassed on several occasions but without effecting an entry into the town.

It was while the new creed was making itself felt in north-east Arabia that Dir'iyyah received its first European visitor. Due to unsettled conditions in Iraq, the trading agency (or Factory, as it was known) of the

British East India Company had moved from Basra in 1793 to Kuwait, to remain there till August 1795. During that time, British help to the Kuwaitis in repelling a Unitarian assault on the town had provoked the Saudis into disrupting the East India Company's desert mail between Basra and Aleppo. In order to try to mend relations with 'Abd al-'Aziz, the head of the British Factory, Samuel Manesty, despatched John Lewis Reinaud to Dir'iyyah, via Qatif and al-Hasa.

Reinaud played a colourful role in the affairs of the British Factory, chiefly in intercepting French despatches, but we do not know the precise substance of his mission to Dir'iyyah, nor its exact date. It probably took place while the Factory was at Kuwait between 1793 and 1795, since it was the disturbance there which prompted the mission. As far as we know Reinaud left no official report, but he did respond to enquiries from the German scholar and agent Seetzen in Aleppo in 1805. This makes it clear that he was in Qatif just before its capture by the Saudis. In a letter to Seetzen Reinaud wrote:

> Drahia [*Dir'iyyah*] is a small town, but beautifully built in the Arabian style. Its position actually makes it a very healthy place to stay. There are several well-cultivated hills around the town, and the whole area is watered by a small river. One finds here some fruit, such as grapes, figs etc., which, I was told, are eaten by all the inhabitants before they are ripe. The Whahabee living in these parts are a very unsophisticated, but on the other hand also a very hospitable people. There are vast numbers of sheep here which are mainly black, have very long fleeces and long ears and produce excellent meat. The horses here are reasonably cheap and the most beautiful in Arabia.
>
> At the time I was staying in Drahia, the name of the shaykh there was Abdil Aziz Ibn Saud, the father of the present shaykh. Saud al Whahabee was the first one to found the new religion and Abdil Aziz simply elaborated it. Abdil Aziz was about sixty years old: a slim, lean man, very educated for a desert Arab. According to reports, his family had about eighty members. He had no court, and all the business went through his hands. A single scribe, called Mullah, was his assistant. In those days his troops numbered about 1000, but now that the Hosiry ['*Asiri*], Aneve ['*Anazah*], Ibn Kalid [*Banu Khalid*], and other Arabian tribes are ruled by him, I am not far wrong if I put the number of his troops, or rather of his subjects who are obliged to take up arms at his command, at 200,000.

The Ottoman Sultan in Istanbul was by now naturally alarmed by developments in eastern Arabia. There was little he could do, however. As he rightly saw, his Empire was in deep decline, enfeebled by war with Russia and internal dissension. Nonetheless, his legitimacy as Caliph and Commander of the Faithful was derived from his claim to be protector of the two Holy Cities of Makkah and Madinah, and he could not ignore the threat emanating from central Arabia. Hence he urged Sulayman Pasha, the Ottoman governor of Baghdad, to stem the rising tide of Saudi power. Sulayman eventually organised an expedition in the winter of 1798-99, an elaborate affair led by Ali Pasha, and directed against Dir'iyyah via Hasa Oasis.

However, the force failed to penetrate beyond al-Hasa. The reasons for its failure were Ali Pasha's incompetent leadership and tactics, and the heroism of the defenders of the Kut in Hofuf and of Qasr Sahud at

This view through an embrasure of Turayf's southern defence tower shows Dir'iyyah's wall across Wadi Hanifah.

Mubarraz just north of Hofuf. The Saudis had been taken by surprise by the rapid advance of the Ottoman force, and there were only a few Najdi fighting men in the Oasis. Some of these retired into the Kut, while about a hundred set about defending Qasr Sahud. Facing an assault by ten to twelve thousand men, albeit badly led, the walls battered by artillery and mined by sappers, they nevertheless held out for two months, when the demoralised Ottoman troops gave up in despair and withdrew. The incident vividly demonstrates the steadfastness of Dir'iyyah's warriors of Islam.

The result was a truce between Dir'iyyah and Baghdad, to be agreed for six years, which was proposed by Ali Pasha while Saud had the retreating Ottoman force at bay at the wells of Thaj. Saud sent an envoy to Sulayman Pasha's court to conclude it. The Englishman Brydges provides a splendid eye-witness report of this encounter, which pointed up the contrast between the direct simplicity of Wahhabi ways and the ostentation of Ottoman diplomacy. The unaccompanied envoy, in his normal attire and sublimely unimpressed by the finery around him, walked with great gravity and dignity through the assembled troops and officials, straight up to where the Pasha was seated, and addressed him with these brief, well-chosen words:

> Hoy Sulayman! Peace be upon all those who think right. 'Abd al-'Aziz has sent me to deliver to you this letter, and to receive from you the ratification of an agreement made between his son, Saud, and your servant Ali; let it be done soon, and in good form; and the curse of God be on him who acts treacherously. If ye seek instruction, 'Abd al-'Aziz will afford it.

The final sentence was no less than a declaration to the Pasha's face of the impurity of his faith. The envoy handed over the letter, written on a small scrap of paper, rose abruptly and left, to the discomfiture of the outraged Pasha, who took the lofty view of the sons of the desert which, since the dawn of civilisation, had often led to the downfall of rulers in the Fertile Crescent. "The Uzbegs are proverbial for bad manners", he is reported to have said, "but the Arabs beat them all to pieces."

After consolidating their position in eastern Arabia, the Saudis extended their influence into the Gulf and south-east Arabia. Using al-Hasa and Buraymi as bases, they enlisted the support of the seafaring Qawasim of Ras al-Khaymah and Sharjah, whose attacks on shipping provoked retaliation by a British fleet from India in 1809. Dir'iyyah also brought Bahrain and Oman into a sporadic tributary relationship, in the process bringing over various Omani tribes to the banner of reform.

By the mid-1790s, the Ottoman Sultan had become equally concerned by the direct threat from Najd to western Arabia and the Holy Cities. Particularly alarming had been an exploratory mission by Saud in 1795 to Turabah, in south-western Najd on the borders of Sharifian influence. The Porte began to put pressure on the Sharif of Makkah, Ghalib ibn Musa'id, to take action against the Wahhabis. Ghalib was a larger-than-life personality who was able to control his Sharifian relatives and sustain a measure of independence in the Hijaz from the Porte. On several occasions his predecessors had refused leave to the Wahhabi puritans of Najd to make the pilgrimage, and the Qadi of Makkah had denounced them as infidels. Ghalib could count upon the loyalty of the Hijazi bedouin tribes, including the 'Utaybah and Buqum of the Najdi borderlands.

However, Ghalib was to maintain an equivocal attitude towards the *muwahhidun*: while hostile to their territorial expansion, he could not deny the purity of their doctrines or their valour in the field. He could therefore often decide that his interests were best served by cooperating with them. Nonetheless, he started confidently, denouncing their ways and, from 1790, conducting raids into al-Qasim, Turabah, Ranyah and Bishah. In 1796, his second expedition into Najd was heavily defeated with great loss of weapons and equipment. Meanwhile Dir'iyyah's allies were probing through Asir towards Najran and the Yemen frontier.

As Dir'iyyah's authority spread, so the tribes of the Hijaz marches, in particular Ghalib's old allies the 'Utaybah and Buqum, began to declare allegiance to it. In 1798 the Sharif Ghalib led a large force to the oases of south-western Najd. After initial successes his army suffered a catastrophic reverse at Khurmah at the hands of the Qahtan, tribal allies of Dir'iyyah. Besides the usual loot of weapons and equipment, a large sum of money fell into Wahhabi hands. As a result of this defeat Ghalib wrote to 'Abd al-'Aziz at Dir'iyyah, proposing peace and inviting him to permit the pilgrimage to be made by his people. A truce was made and, in 1799, a great pilgrim caravan made its way across Najd. In 1800, Saud himself with a large number of his men made the pilgrimage.

For two years there was peace in the west, and the truce with Baghdad held in the north-east. Dir'iyyah's writ ran in all of Najd and al-Hasa, and along much of the Gulf coast. Northwards, expansion continued. The Wahhabis had taken al-Jawf in the late 1790s, and raided into Shararat country on the Syrian border. Further raids followed into the Iraqi marches, after which Saud defeated a large force of Shammar and Zafir bedouin.

Below: **The Englishman Harford Jones Brydges (centre), whose *Brief History of the Wahauby* is an important contemporary source, is depicted here on a mission to the court of Persia.**

In April 1801 the usual skirmishing with the Muntafiq and Zafir was followed by a dramatic new turn of events. It was said that the Muntafiq were to blame for breaking the truce between Baghdad and Dir'iyyah. Whatever the case, a caravan of Persian pilgrims was attacked and plundered by the Wahhabis, and then Saud, at the head of an army of twelve thousand men, suddenly appeared before Karbala, the Iraqi city sacred to Shi'ah Muslims. In the eyes of Saud's men Karbala represented a prime hotbed of heresy, but its attractions were increased by its richly endowed tombs which were centres of Shiite pilgrimage. Regarding their truce with the Pashaliq of Baghdad as null and void, they fell upon Karbala, assaulting its walls, entering the city and destroying its shrines. When they left, at least three thousand people lay massacred in its streets. It was a tempting target, and an untold quantity of booty was taken back to Dir'iyyah. Sulayman Pasha, on being told the news of Karbala, is reported to have said, "It is not fit that I should live longer." A few months later, he died.

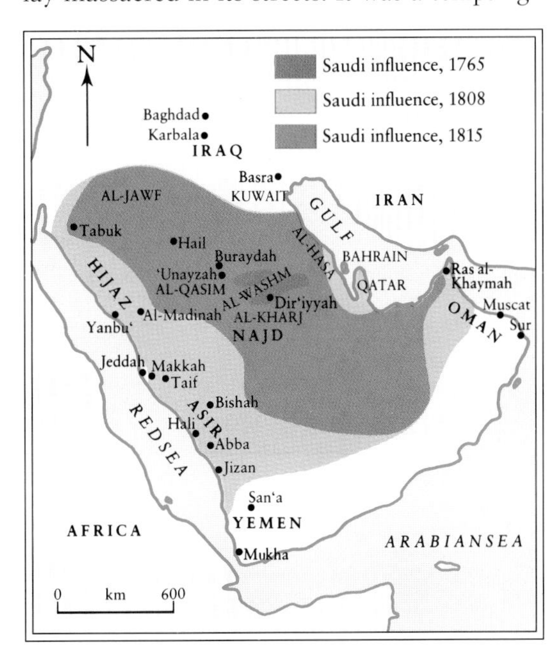

Karbala illustrated the strengths and short-comings of the reform movement. In a way it was a classic tribal raid writ large. Once a battle was won outside their own territory the Wahhabis had little desire – and only rudimentary mechanisms – for permanent occupation. A campaign to spread their message by winning hearts and minds would have been more effective. As it was, their aim was plunder rather than conversion. Yet the Wahhabi warriors' invincibility was derived from the new unity of purpose inspired by their creed. The principles of *jihad* added a very different element to desert warfare: slaughter without quarter was now the order of the day. Intolerance masqueraded as virtue, as it has for many movements in history which have believed themselves to be the sole possessors of the truth. The distinction between plundering and propagating the faith too easily became blurred in the heat of battle.

Karbala sent a shock-wave around the Muslim world. A second expedition against Dir'iyyah was organised from Iraq under the Muntafiq chief Thuwayni, the old ally of the Banu Khalid. Thuwayni was assassinated before his army reached much beyond Kuwait, and his remaining troops were put to flight by Saud, whose men captured the entire enemy camp and weaponry.

As if Karbala were not enough, and at about the same time, hostilities with Sharif Ghalib were re-kindled. Hali on the Red Sea coast changed hands three times. In 1802 Taif was taken with the collaboration of 'Uthman al-Mudhayfi, a brother-in-law of Ghalib, and another, albeit much smaller, massacre took place. 'Uthman was installed as Saudi governor and went on to take the Red Sea port of Qunfudhah. Encouraged by this, Saud led an army towards Makkah. Ghalib and the Makkans withstood a siege of several months before he was forced to abandon the city for Jeddah. In April 1803 the Unitarians donned pilgrim garments and entered the town peaceably. Once there, they performed the little pilgrimage in the prescribed fashion. They then turned to the task of cleansing the city – that is, demolishing every shrine and commemorative building which offended against their creed. Saud prohibited the mention of the Ottoman Sultan's name in public prayers, and the musicians accompanying the Egyptian and Syrian *mahmal*s were banned. A *qadi* from Dir'iyyah was appointed.

The entry into Makkah is recorded in an eye-witness account by one of the divines of Dir'iyyah, Abdullah ibn Muhammad ibn 'Abd al-Wahhab. A son of the Shaykh, he wrote it on the spot in April 1803. Abdullah was one of the many Wahhabi divines and members of Al Saud who were to be put to death in 1818 by Ibrahim Pasha when the latter took Dir'iyyah. The tone of his report powerfully conveys the zeal and sense of commitment of Dir'iyyah's soldiers of reform, and the efforts of the reformers to convince the Makkan establishment of the purity of their doctrines:

> Praise be to God, the Lord of the Universe, and blessing and peace be upon our Prophet Muhammad, the faithful, and on his people and his companions, and those who lived after them, and their successors of the next generation! Now I was engaged in the holy war, carried on by those who truly believe in the unity of God, when God, praised be He, graciously permitted us to enter Makkah, the

holy, the exalted, at midday, on the 6th day of the week, on the 8th of the month (Muharram), 1218, Hijri. Before this, Saud, our leader in the holy war, whom the Lord protect, had summoned the nobles, the divines, and the common people of Makkah; for indeed the leaders of the pilgrims and the rulers of Makkah had resolved on battle, and had risen up against us in the Holy Place (Haram), to exclude us from the house of God. But when the army of the true believers advanced, the Lord filled their hearts with terror, and they fled hither and thither. Then our commander gave protection to every one within the Holy Place, while we, with shaven heads and hair cut short, entered with safety, crying "Labbaika", without fear of any created being, and only of the Lord God. Now, though we were more numerous, better armed and disciplined than the people of Makkah, yet we did not cut down their trees, neither did we hunt, nor shed any blood except the blood of victims, and of those four-footed beasts which the Lord has made lawful by His commands.

When our pilgrimage was over, we gathered the people together ... and our leader, whom the Lord save, explained to the divines what we required of the people, and for which we would slay them, viz., a pure belief in the Unity of God Almighty. He pointed out to them that there was no dispute between us and them except on two points, and that one of these was a sincere belief in the Unity of God. ... The second point related to actions lawful and unlawful as prohibited. ...

Then they jointly and severally admitted that our belief was best, and promised the Amir to be guided by the Quran and the Sunnat. He accepted their promise and pardoned them. Neither did he give any of them the least annoyance, nor cease to treat them with the greatest friendship, especially the divines. ... Moreover, we explained to them what the Amir had spoken to them publicly, and pointed out the proofs of it in the Quran and Sunnat, and in the conduct of our spotless ancestors, such as the orthodox Caliphs who ruled over their followers. ... Again we pointed out to them that we were searchers after the truth wheresoever it might be. ... In fine, they were not able to chide us for a single thing ...

Left: **The tower, crenellations and firing-step on the main oasis wall in Jabal Qurayn have recently been restored.**

When this was over, we razed all the large tombs in the city which the people generally worshipped and believed in, and by which they hoped to obtain benefits or ward off evil, so that there did not remain an idol to be adored in that pure city, for which God be praised. Then the taxes and customs we abolished, all the different kinds of instruments for using tobacco we destroyed, and tobacco itself we proclaimed forbidden. Next we burned the dwellings of those selling hashish, and living in open wickedness, and issued a proclamation, directing the people to constantly exercise themselves in prayer. ...

We appointed a ruler over them, 'Abd al-Mu'in, the Sharif, [*Sharif Ghalib's brother*] and his rule was established without shedding of blood, and without dishonouring or annoying any person ... Afterwards we gave them a pamphlet, composed by Shaykh Muhammad on the Unity of God ...

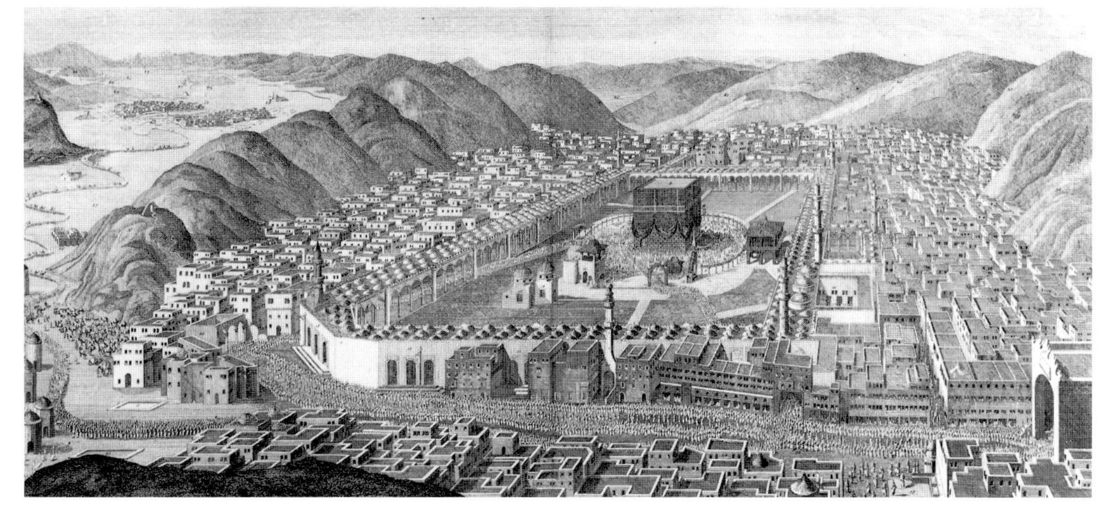

Below left: **This European engraving of Makkah, showing the Ka'bah, Haram and pilgrims, was done in 1803, the year that the Imam Saud and the soldiers of Dir'iyyah took over the Holy City.**

Right: **This viewpoint commands Wadi Hanifah from Turayf, just west of the Faisal Tower on the right.**

Daily life quickly returned to normal: the shops are said to have opened for business as usual the next day. As soon as he could Saud marched on Jeddah. However, Jeddah was well defended, and was easily supplied by sea. Saud abandoned the attempt after a short siege and returned to Najd. Ghalib re-took Makkah immediately but was careful to maintain an outward adherence to reformist doctrines, and waived customs dues at Jeddah for all true Wahhabis. But Sultan Selim III's prestige as Commander of the Faithful and Servant of the Two Holy Places had been damaged. A further blow to his standing was the disruption to the pilgrimage. The regular *haj* caravans from Cairo and Damascus no longer set out, though individual pilgrims were never prevented as long as they conducted themselves according to Wahhabi precepts.

Later in 1803 'Abd al-'Aziz, now 82 years old, was assassinated in the mosque at Dir'iyyah. The assassin was alleged to be bent on revenge for the loss of relatives in the sack of Karbala. Saud had already been named some years previously as his father's successor. His mother was a daughter of Shaykh Muhammad ibn 'Abd al Wahhab, so he combined political with religious legitimacy. Renowned in the years before his father's death for his generalship, Saud was to become equally revered for the sternness and justice of his government. Deservedly known by his people as "the Great" he combined, in the Najdi tradition of rulership, great authority with unpretentiousness of manner and direct accessibility to his people.

A vivid portrait of the man emerges from the works of Ibn Bishr, the mysterious Spanish traveller Ali Bey and Jean Louis Burckhardt. Interviews given to the Swiss traveller Charles Didier in 1854 by one of Saud's sons, Khalid, who was then living in exile in Jeddah, are also an important source. By Didier's time, Khalid ibn Saud had himself briefly been Imam of Riyadh in 1840-1, under Egyptian tutelage, before being forced into exile.

According to this account, the Imam Saud was a very handsome man, with a voice so gentle that all his words went straight to the heart. He was popularly known as "Father of Moustaches" (Abu Shuwarib), because of the luxuriant growth on his upper lip. He put all his own precepts into practice: he wore a simple *abaya* of wool that contained no silk, and set an example of all the patriarchal virtues. Every evening, in his palace, he conducted family devotions. The Swiss Didier notes the similarity here to many protestant families. The palace was always full of people, from the highest to the lowest, who came to discuss their affairs with him and to eat at his house as if it were their own. He was greeted by all on the basis of complete equality. Affable in his manners, he would insist that everyone remain seated in his presence. As prudent in counsel as he was skilful and resolute in application, he dispensed justice to all with incorruptible impartiality and inflexible rigour. The integrity of the judges he sent out to the settlements was still proverbial in Arabia in Didier's time. Capital punishment was used sparingly, but a disgrace feared almost as much as death itself was the shaving of the beard of the guilty party. Himself loyal to his word, he had a horror of deceit and would sometimes flog liars, but as soon as he felt anger flare up within him he would ask his aides to restrain him, and would later thank those who had done so. Eloquent and well-read in the Muslim scriptures beyond most *'ulama'*, he willingly took part in religious controversies and, while expounding with zeal, would allow others to do the same. Saud's only luxury was his horses, of which he had more than two thousand – according to Burckhardt the finest stud of horses in the entire East. He also kept fast riding camels.

However, there are signs that in some ways Saud did not quite measure up to the ideal of the Unitarian Imam. He was still enough the traditional ruler to be criticised for his single perceived vice, of which he himself was conscious – that of avarice. Burckhardt notes

that Saud's reputation for avarice grew with his years in power, and a note of disapproval is clear in Ibn Bishr's description of him: he makes much of Saud's taste for luxury, which he contrasts with his father's austerity. He tells us that Saud dressed in fine and sometimes colourful clothes, and his sword

Far left and centre: **The street between Sa'd's and Nasr's Palaces gives some idea of Dir'iyyah in its heyday.**

Left: **The restored Mosque of Subalat Mudi with its simple *mihrab* (*right*) demonstrates the reform movement's stylistic austerity.**

was decorated with gold and precious stones. Saud greatly extended his father's palace to accommodate his wives, whose clothes were also of rich materials – even of silk, despite the Wahhabi prohibition. They had a vast amount of jewelry. Saud was fond of good food and imported cooks from Qatif to satisfy his tastes. His son the future Imam Abdullah took after his father in his taste for luxury. Despite the fabled sternness of the two men, something of the austerity which one feels would have been insisted upon by Shaykh Muhammad ibn 'Abd al Wahhab, had he been alive, seems to have been lost.

Saud ruled until his death in 1814, and his reign marks the zenith of the Saudi "empire" in Arabia. Madinah and Yanbu' were taken in 1804. The Prophet's tomb was stripped of its treasure – much of this was dispersed, but some, such as priceless Qur'ans with gem-encrusted bindings, was taken back to Dir'iyyah – and the same measures taken as at Makkah, except that tribute was exacted from its people. After his accession, Saud avoided endangering himself in the field, but the raiding continued, especially on Turkish Iraq where, led by Saud's son the future Imam Abdullah, the Najdis experienced several reverses. In the south-west the southern Wahhabis had better success under their leaders: Abu Nuqtah, the principal shaykh of Asir, overran the entire Red Sea coast between Qunfudhah and Hudaydah, setting in train a vigorous trading relationship between Yemen and Najd.

The Sharif Ghalib, caught between the conflicting demands of the new movement and his Ottoman overlords, continued his policy of trying to please whichever seemed most immediately threatening. Although he retained his title, he had lost control of Madinah; in Makkah he had to share his authority with Dir'iyyah, and then only on condition of his strict observance of reformist tenets. He held sway only in Jeddah, where he recognised, as in the past, the nominal authority of the Ottoman Sultan. But even in Jeddah he was vulnerable, as Wahhabi war parties frequently assaulted the city.

When Saud arrived to make the pilgrimage, Ghalib showered him and his entourage with gifts – by which Saud professed to be embarrassed. The reformers imposed their strict disciplines on the pilgrimage and, in one instance in 1807, showed their commitment by turning back the Syrian pilgrim caravan at Madinah. Led by Saud, they went on to perform their own *haj* in great numbers. In February 1807, after the *haj*, Saud issued an order clearing Makkah and Madinah of all Sharif Ghalib's and the Ottoman Sultan's troops and *qadis*, so tightening his grip on the Hijaz. Dir'iyyah had asserted its claim to be rightful Guardian of the Holy Cities of Islam.

The pilgrimage of 1807 took place under the shrewd eye of the cultivated Spanish Muslim traveller Ali Bey al-'Abbasi. His account evokes the uneasy atmosphere in Makkah under the shared authority of Sharif Ghalib and the Imam Saud. "It results, from these conflicts of power, that the poor inhabitants know not who is their true master", he remarked. When the pilgrims from Dir'iyyah entered Makkah that year he saw five or six thousand of them thronging the streets of Makkah "without any other covering than a small piece of cloth round their waist, except some few who had a napkin placed upon the left shoulder, that passed under the right arm, being naked in every other respect, with their matchlocks upon their shoulders, and their khanjears or large knives hung to their girdles." At the sight of the torrent of semi-naked armed men the terrified Makkans fled and hid, while the pilgrims entered the Haram in zealous confusion, shouting prayers and jostling each other, to the despair of their leaders and guides, and swarmed round the Ka'bah like bees.

He noted admiringly that these men of Dir'iyyah were physically very well made, though short in stature. He was particularly impressed by some of their heads, which were so handsome that "they might have been compared with Apollo, Antinous or the Gladiator. They have very lively eyes, the nose and mouth well formed, fine teeth, and very expressive countenances." Though they presented a ferocious aspect, their discipline was above reproach. The Sharif Ghalib hid himself and manned all his forts, but this according to Ali Bey was unnecessary. He saw Saud the Great's camp at Muna, and was present as the Imam led 45,000 Wahhabi pilgrims on the plain of Arafat for the climax of the *haj*.

MUHAMMAD ALI'S EXPEDITION TO THE HIJAZ, 1811-15

With the loss of the Holy Cities in 1803-4, Sultan Selim had inevitably become more than ever anxious to suppress the reform movement. The Ottoman Empire's fortunes had sunk low with the occupation of Egypt by Napoleon in 1798, but Egypt had been restored to it by the Treaty of Paris in 1802. Selim III was the first Sultan to become concerned about the Empire's decline relative to the European powers, and set in hand a programme of modernisation of the army. The pursuit of this New Order led to his deposition in 1807.

By then Muhammad Ali was emerging as the real master of Egypt. Of Albanian origin, Muhammad Ali had started out as an officer in the Ottoman army, and had contrived in the chaos after Napoleon's occupation to rise to power over the Mamluk beys who were Egypt's traditional rulers. He was ruthless, ambitious and modernising, and aimed to make Egypt independent while, for the time being, posing as the faithful servant of his Ottoman overlord, the Caliph and "Shadow of God upon Earth". Sultan Selim and his successor Mahmoud II (reigned 1808-39), another reforming Sultan, saw an Arabian campaign conducted by Muhammad Ali as a means simultaneously of restoring their prestige and of sapping the growing power of the over-ambitious new governor of Egypt.

Hence they had been urging Muhammad

Ali, since 1807, to intervene in the Hijaz. Muhammad Ali was eager to use such an intervention to increase his power and standing, but not until he had consolidated his position in Egypt against his Mamluk opposition. The moment of decision came with a great Saudi raid into Syria in 1810, with their allies the Ruwala, which threatened Damascus. Using this event to extract a loan from the anxious Sultan, Muhammad Ali prepared a great expedition. In 1811 he placed his eighteen-year-old son Tusun in command, and sent the fleet off to Yanbu'. As he did so, he slaughtered his last Mamluk opponents in the citadel in Cairo.

Tusun's first target was Madinah, but he suffered a crushing defeat on the way there at Judaydah, at the hands of Saud's sons Abdullah and Faisal with their allies of the Harb tribe. Reinforced, Tusun finally went on to take Madinah at the end of 1812. Sharif Ghalib then let him into Makkah, and together they attacked and entered Taif. But Ghalib was, as ever, unable to make up his mind whether his best interests lay with Dir'iyyah or the Ottomans. His real design was to let the Turco-Egyptian force and the Saudis weaken each other. Because of this he was distrusted by Muhammad Ali, and he was soon to lose everything.

For, in 1813, Muhammad Ali himself came to the Hijaz. He made Makkah his headquarters, and contrived to kidnap the temporising Ghalib and remove him into exile. He saw success in the Hijaz as vital to his career, as his position in Egypt was still precarious and he was mistrusted by the Sultan in Istanbul. He dealt astutely with the tribes and took care to restore security in the Hijaz. With Tusun's recovery of the Holy Cities, the *haj* caravan had arrived from Cairo with all its former pomp at the end of 1812, and in 1813 the Syrian one came for the first time in ten years. Pilgrims once more flocked to the Holy Places without fear of reformist strictures. But Muhammad Ali still needed to take two important centres of the southern Wahhabis: the oasis of Turabah in south-western Najd, which was well placed to threaten Makkah, and the Red Sea port of Qunfudhah.

Sharif Ghalib's supporters had taken refuge with the southern Wahhabis at Turabah, among the Buqum. Here a woman, Ghaliyyah, had achieved the distinction, unique in Islamic Arabia, of being recognised as leader. Through a combination of sound judgment and her reputation among the Egyptian soldiery as a sorceress, she defeated the force sent out under Tusun in late 1813, inflicting heavy losses on it. In 1814 Muhammad Ali sent his governor of Jeddah, Zaim-Oglu, with 3200 men to take Qunfudhah. Zaim-Oglu occupied it without a struggle, but unfortunately the town's wells were three hours march away, and in Wahhabi hands. Ten thousand Wahhabi warriors swept down upon the port and the Turks fled in panic to their boats. Few escaped.

Just as things became desperate for Muhammad Ali, Saud the Great died, in May 1814, at the age of sixty-eight, and was succeeded by his son Abdullah. His last words to Abdullah were said to have been that he should "never engage the Egyptians in the open plain."

This was sound advice from a successful and experienced commander, but it was promptly ignored. Saud's death brought a change in fortunes for the Egyptians. Muhammad Ali, never one to be discouraged, rallied, courting tribal chiefs and calling in more troops and equipment. In January 1815 he took the field himself. At Bisal, near Taif, he lured a large Wahhabi force down from the mountains and onto the plain by pretending to flee. It was an old trick, but it often worked. The slaughter was great. After the battle, Burckhardt tells us, whole lines of bedouin fighters, roped together by their legs, were found dead, having sworn to their women at parting that they would never flee before a Turk. Faisal, brother of the new Imam Abdullah, was present, and the defeat sounded the alarm in Dir'iyyah.

The strongholds of the southern Wahhabis – Turabah, Bishah, Ranyah and Qunfudhah – soon capitulated. Bisal marked the turning-point in the war in the Hijaz. The Wahhabis were cut off from the Red Sea, and the Egyptians were soon ready to go on the offensive into Najd. Muhammad Ali returned to Makkah and thence to Madinah, where he had appointed his son Tusun as governor.

Muhammad Ali presides over the massacre of the last Mamluk *beys* in the Citadel at Cairo in 1811.

CHAPTER SIX

Seat of Government

The apogee of the empire

THE SETTLEMENTS OF DIR'IYYAH

Dir'iyyah is the name not of a single settlement, but of an area of settlement and agriculture – a wadi-based oasis – on either side of an eight-kilometre stretch of Wadi Hanifah. The northern limits of the oasis were the villages of 'Ilb and 'Awdah, situated among the palms on the west bank. Below these, on the east bank, stood the major settlement of Ghasibah, opposite the tributary of Bulaydah. Here Wadi Hanifah bears eastwards, and the left bank below Ghasibah was lined with a series of farming settlements extending past the cliff of Turayf on the opposite bank. One of these settlements, right opposite Turayf, was distinctive: named Bujayri, it was where Shaykh Muhammad ibn 'Abd al-Wahhab resided with his family and disciples. Some of the other villages are named by the local historian Ibn Bishr: apart from Turayf, Ghasibah and Bujayri, he mentions Sahl, Zuhayrah, Malwi, Naqib and Surayhah.

East of Turayf, the wadi is forced to make a sharp turn to the south-west by the high cliff of Qurayn. The southern side of the Turayf bluff is bounded by the large tributary, Sha'ib Safar, which joins Wadi Hanifah opposite a pass descending the cliff of Qurayn, Nazlat al-Nasiriyyah. This was the main route to Riyadh. Just beyond the pass, on the left bank, lies the extensive, fertile farming area of Mulaybid, marking the end of the oasis.

In its heyday in the 18th and early 19th centuries the ruling clan of the House of Saud made the naturally defended site of Turayf their centre of government and, as their power and prosperity grew, developed it with imposing palaces and other buildings. Turayf is the site which visitors to Dir'iyyah see today. The majestic palaces of the Imams and princes were built in a distinctive and confident style which seems to have no survivor in Najd after their abandonment in 1818-21 – "the noblest monument in all Wahhabiland," as Philby called them in 1917.

The Imams also fortified the entire oasis with a wall, with bastions at intervals, running along the heights on either side of the wadi. This has been restored today by the Department of Antiquities, and is an impressive reminder of the scale of settlement at Dir'iyyah. Ibn Bishr makes particular mention of the separate fortified enclosure of Zahra Samhan with its own bastions and gates, and the Ghasibah fort nearby, both of which were to feature in the siege in 1818.

Two 19th century French scholars, the geographer Jomard and the historian Mengin, collected information from Najdi informants in Cairo and from eye-witnesses who had taken part in the siege of Dir'iyyah. They put its adult population at 13,000, and correctly recognised that it was a scatter of settlements:

> Dereyah comprises five small towns, each one surrounded by a wall fortified with bastions at intervals; besides this there was a good strong fort which defended the quarter known as Ghacybeh, as well as Tourfiyeh. Both of these places were situated near a mountain. Abdullah ibn Saud lived in Tureyf; Sahl was separated from Tureyf only by the torrent bed of the Batn [*i.e. Wadi Hanifah*]. Kosscyrein [*Qusayrayn*] extended through the middle of the gardens: its inhabitants had no means of defence and so used to retire, at the beginning of the siege, into the other parts of the town.

An earlier French writer, Corancez, who was an official at the French embassy in Damascus and published a book about the Wahhabis in 1810, knew that Dir'iyyah comprised at least two main settlements, Turayf where the Al Saud lived, and Bujayri, on the opposite bank of the Wadi Hanifah, where the religious leader had his abode. Bujayri contained twenty-eight mosques and thirty colleges, and its location right opposite Turayf seems to identify it with, or at least make it adjacent to, the Sahl mentioned by Mengin and the Selle recorded by Sadleir. Corancez does not mention the old and important town of Ghasibah or any of the other settlements.

Corancez, having first confusingly stated that Dir'iyyah was a town built of stone, estimated that there were some two and a half thousand houses in Dir'iyyah, which he accurately describes as built of stone and mud brick. Dir'iyyah's markets were composed of easily transportable reed stalls. There were no public cafés – which seems a typically French observation. He also states that there were no public baths and that the town was not fortified. Both these comments seem odd in view of the surviving remains of elaborate fortifications and the well-known bath house. But it may have been the case that fortifications were much less developed before the threat of Ibrahim Pasha's campaign, and that the baths were built late in the town's history, during the reign of Saud the Great or Abdullah. Corancez concludes with the unchallengeable information that Wadi Hanifah ran through the settlement and there were gardens all around growing dates, apricots, peaches, watermelons, wheat, barley and millet.

Ibn Bishr tells us that the people of Dir'iyyah used to live in low-built houses with many rooms surrounding a courtyard. They had plenty of furniture and even the poor people had many carpets. Ordinary people did not use beds, while the rulers used wooden beds. Bed covers were customarily of wool or, very occasionally, stuffed with cotton. Dishes were made of copper and cups of wood, and they used to spread their meals on the floor on a large circular piece of leather, men and women eating separately.

Ibn Bishr emphasises the lively commercial activity at Dir'iyyah. The people made a good living from trade with neighbouring countries, exporting horses, camels and dates in exchange for cloth, silk, copper, weapons and coffee. Its merchants travelled to Syria, Egypt, Yemen, Iran and Turkey. Merchandise was stored not in warehouses, but in the merchants' houses.

Dir'iyyah's commercial prominence meant that house prices were three to twenty times as high as elsewhere in Najd. The expansion of the population had brought about a building boom which had caused a wood shortage. While many of the people owned farms and gardens, Ibn Bishr tells us that there were also specialist artisans such as sword, dagger and spear manufacturers, saddle-makers, carpenters, jewellers and tailors. Firearms too were manufactured – more probably they were imported and then adapted to the local style – and a very good type of gunpowder was made at Dir'iyyah. Ibn Bishr says that the method of making gunpowder was an Iranian one brought to Dir'iyyah by Shaykh Muhammad ibn 'Abd al-Wahhab himself.

The economic effects of Dir'iyyah's rise to power were profound. A normally subsistence-based Najdi farming community, whose people were traditionally self-sufficient, had quickly evolved into a cash economy with a good number of specialist artisans producing for home consumption and export. Large classes of people were involved full-time in the business of the ruling household, the ruler's bodyguard and religious instruction, all non-productive activities which created a strong demand for imports. Like 'Uyaynah before it and Riyadh after it, Dir'iyyah had become untypical of Najdi settlements.

"AN EARLY NINETEENTH CENTURY CAMERA"

"AN EARLY NINETEENTH CENTURY CAMERA"

There is no visual record of Dir'iyyah in its heyday. Nor is it known with complete certainty what its buildings looked like before they fell into ruin, though reconstructions such as the Palace of Sa'd, the Palace of Nasr, the Faisal Tower and the walls of Turayf are very plausible attempts to recreate their original appearance.

However, early 20th century photographs of daily life in Najd portray a society that had changed little for hundreds of years. By combining some of these images in photomontages with photographs of locations in Turayf today, and paying close attention to contemporary descriptions, we can conjure up something close to a picture of daily life in Dir'iyyah.

Although the dress of the people was essentially similar in its simplicity to that of more recent times, there seems to have been one significant difference. The *'iqal*, or rope headband holding in place the *kufiyyah* or headcloth, appears not to have been worn. Instead, notables would wind around their *kufiyyah* a piece of cloth woven with narrow strips of red, or sometimes even a cashmere shawl. *Kufiyyah*s themselves seem to have been plain. Silk in any form was strictly forbidden. Otherwise, the familiar *thawb*, a robe reaching to just above the ankles, sometimes with the black *abaya* or cloak over it, was worn by men. Women went veiled.

The contemporary engraving of the Imam Abdullah ibn Saud in 1818, shown on p.64, is a valuable record of the style of dress in the First Saudi State.

The view from a typical domestic courtyard in Turayf.

DIR'IYYAH AS CAPITAL

The fundamental aim of reform at Dir'iyyah was the creation of an Islamic state based on Shari'ah law rather than on custom and tribal traditions. The principles of the new state were intended to encompass not only the settled people of the towns and villages, but also the nomads. These principles entailed that the ruler of the state was transformed from a tribal chief into a political and spiritual leader – an Imam rather than an amir – who could ensure that the teachings of Shaykh Muhammad ibn 'Abd al-Wahhab found expression in the institutions of society and the practices of everyday life. The Imam's legitimacy was founded on his acceptance by his people and his willingness to consult the *'ulama'* and leading citizens. The Imam was, hence, far from an arbitrary ruler. His position was conceived as an equal partnership in government with the *'ulama'*, whose role was to advise him on what was best for the community under God. In return for fulfilling his obligations in upholding God's law and working for the community's welfare, the ruler was owed the support of the *'ulama'* and the obedience of his people.

Amongst the bedouin tribes the establishment of a central authority brought a cessation of feuding, which was replaced by a system of centrally administered justice. In tribe and settlement the order went out that all public disputes should be brought before the Imam in Dir'iyyah, so curtailing the role of customary law. Punishment was handed out strictly and impartially, and usually took the form of fines levied in kind. Capital punishment was rare. Such was the new state of law and order under Saudi rule that, for the first time, people could travel without fear of depredation by bedouin. State-inflicted punishments were substituted for private vendetta, and there was a system of state compensation for losses. In the Holy Cities the *muwahhidun*, though feared, were respected for their good faith and adherence to promises and agreements.

Tribal shaykhs were allowed to keep their hereditary rights provided that they adhered to reformist doctrines, paid their taxes and levied the fighters required of them. The desert was at peace. An enormous amount of energy previously spent on inter-tribal feuding was harnessed to a larger ideal – that of the Muslim community. The towns and settled folk benefited from the peace, and merchants were able to carry on their business in unprecedented safety. As Burckhardt noted, the pillars of the new order were taxation, military conscription, internal peace, and the rigid administration of justice. A sovereign state was being forged where before had been warring tribes and communities.

The relationship between ruler and religious adviser was never better illustrated than by that between Saud's father 'Abd al-'Aziz and the Shaykh himself. We are told that 'Abd al-'Aziz, like his own father Muhammad ibn Saud, never undertook an enterprise without the Shaykh's agreement. As it was said, no camel-riders were sent out without first consulting him. All opinions and statements made by them were based on the Shaykh's statements and thinking. All state revenues, including the *zakah* or alms tax, and

one fifth of booty, were handed over to the Shaykh to dispense at his discretion.

The Shaykh was also responsible for the legal system - the appointment of *qadi*s (judges) and *mutawwi*'s. These officers were instruments of the rule of law and the central administration of justice. They were sent to all the settlements, and saw to the observance of moral and religious precepts, such as full public attendance at the five daily prayers, and the banning of evil acts such as drinking alcohol, smoking tobacco, wearing silk clothes or gold jewelry, and music. Punishment for lapses could be swift and harsh.

The First Saudi State represented a remarkable embodiment of the principle of equal partnership between ruler and religious advisers. The theory of this partnership traced its origins to early Islam, during the Abbasid period, but it had perhaps never been so fully put into practice as at Dir'iyyah. When the Shaykh died in 1792, his mantle passed to his four sons, all eminent religious scholars, and he left behind a thriving intellectual tradition dedicated to the propagation of Reform.

The very isolation of Najd from outside influences, and the cultural homogeneity of its people, together meant that an ideology requiring such

Dir'iyyah had several markets, some of them specialised ones for gold, weapons, meat, horses, camels and other livestock. The markets were in open spaces, allowing caravans to pass through. The main market was probably in the bed of the Wadi Hanifah – accessible to merchants and, like many Arabian markets, outside the town. It was thronged with a cosmopolitan crowd of merchants from Yemen, the Hijaz, Bahrain, Oman, Syria and Egypt. Shop rents were high. Many different types of coinage were in circulation (coins were not minted at Dir'iyyah), only Turkish coins not being acceptable. Corancez tells us that the market stalls were lightweight and portable, as shown here. Ibn Bishr compares the hubbub of the buying and selling to the roar of flood-waters coming down from the mountains.

rigid conformity could quickly take root and come to command the fierce allegiance of the entire community. Such a system demands of its adherents the conviction that theirs is the only right way to organise the community under God. There could be no room for the toleration of differences. Once the movement sought to expand, and came up against other beliefs and practices, the inevitable result was intolerance and bloodshed.

As we have seen, Shaykh Muhammad ibn 'Abd al-Wahhab lived on the opposite bank of the wadi from Turayf, in the settlement known as Bujayri. Here he had his mosque, where the handsome new mud-built Najdi mosque stands today. And here he gathered his followers – the scholars and *'ulama'*, several of whom were his own sons and who went on to play a central part in the subsequent evolution of Saudi society.

The religious atmosphere at Dir'iyyah in the time of the Imam Saud is dramatically depicted by Ibn Bishr. Every day a public study group was conducted in the large open space outside the *qasr*, so that everyone would have a chance to attend and to hear the exposition of the Holy Qur'an.

> At sunrise, the people of Dir'iyyah would sit down to study in the inner place known as al-Mawsim, where buying and selling take place. If it was in the summer, then this would be by the shops to the east. If it was winter, then it would be by the shops to the west. A large number of people would assemble, one group after another, and more than could be counted, and the centre of the assembly would be left free for Saud and his relatives and the sons of the Shaykh. Then the sons of the Shaykh would come and sit down, and his uncle and son and brothers, and each of them would come with a retinue and with servants, and would sit down next to the sons of the Shaykh. Then the sons of Saud would come, one after another, and each of them with a large following of prominent people and a retinue and servants. If one of them came to a group which did not rise to their feet out of respect, then they were displeased. When the people had assembled together, then Saud came out of the Qasr with his suite and with a great clamour like the sound of fire on dry wood, which was the noise of swords clashing together because of the intense crowding of people. You could only rarely see a fair-skinned man, for they were all Saud's black slaves. They had valuable swords decorated with gold and silver. Saud was in the midst of them, like a moon appearing in a gap in the clouds. When he came to the assembly, the people in his way would stand up in respect ... until he reached his place and said "Peace be on you" to everyone. Then he would sit down beside Abdullah, the son of the Shaykh, who was responsible for reading the Qur'an at that study ... When the study was finished, Saud would stand up and go into the Qasr in one of the rooms near to the people, and they would bring their needs to him until the sun was high in the sky and the time came for the midday rest ...

The Imam used the *qasr* itself to receive his people – the audience hall which can still be entered among the Salwa Palaces. Here he heard their petitions and dispensed hospitality and largesse to his many guests. All three functions were central to the role of the Saudi ruler. Much of the information on Dir'iyyah recorded by Burckhardt, during his travels in the Hijaz in 1814-16, centres on the *qasr*. According to him, this seat of government was spacious, though without any splendid apartments. He also tells us:

> [*Saud*] resided with all his family in a large mansion built by his father on the declivity of the mountain, a little above the town of Derayeh. All his children, with their families, and all his brothers had their separate apartments in that building ... In his house he kept his treasures, and received all those who came on business to Derayeh. There the great emirs, or chiefs of considerable tribes, were lodged and feasted on their arrival, while people of inferior rank resided with their acquaintances in the town; but if they came on business they might dine or sup at the chief's house, and bring from it a daily allowance of food for their horses and camels. It may easily be conceived, that the palace was constantly full of guests.

Burckhardt estimated the number of household members and guests on a daily basis to be 400 to 500 – a tremendous strain on any ruler's commissariat, but an obligation he could not evade without forfeiting his authority and credibility. Ibn Bishr describes the daily business of feeding this multitude:

> As for his conduct with guests, his treasurer told me that there would issue from his stores each day 500 measures of wheat and rice. The guest-officer responsible would invite the guests to dine from after noon-day until after the last evening prayer. The first to come in would have meat and rice and bread to eat. Those who came after them would have nearly the same, while the rest would just have wheat.

By Saud's reign (1803-1814) the influx of tax revenues from most of Arabia and booty from campaigns had brought a prosperity to Dir'iyyah which was unprecedented for a Najdi town. This prosperity was underpinned by the military successes of the state. A chief obligation of towns and tribes who had sworn allegiance to Dir'iyyah was the provision of men for the army. Apart from the ruler's bodyguard, which in Saud's time was a much-feared élite corps of three hundred horsemen in armour, there was no standing army, and troops had to be levied on a campaign-by-campaign basis at pre-arranged gathering points. The ruler would send a written order to each district, requiring it to furnish a contingent in proportion to its population and the gravity of the situation. All males between the ages of 18 and 60 were liable for service. When a full call-up went out, specific numbers were not usually requisitioned: all who possessed a riding camel were obliged to attend. On such occasions the chief would say, ominously, "We shall not count those who join the army, but those who stay behind."

The campaigning force so formed would consist of some cavalry, who were provided with horses, fodder and a salary; camel-riders who had to bring weapons and provisions and did not receive any pay; foot-soldiers with matchlocks who rode camels on campaign; and the bodyguard, who were supported entirely by the ruler. When riding on campaign, one camel would frequently carry two riders. Horses were not ridden until the order came to ride into battle, to keep them fresh. Among the camel-riders and foot-soldiers only the impoverished would be assisted by the wealthy of their communities, or by the public treasury.

The numbers of fighting men available to the Saudi Imam increased steadily with the expansion of the Saudi domain, it was said from a mere seven camel-riders in the very early days to some 100,000 or more at its height. Their military superiority derived from their zeal, energy, orderliness and obedience to their commanders, all qualities which were to be reflected a century or so later in the Ikhwan fighters of Ibn Saud. These qualities brought them overwhelming successes in the field, and led to the myth of their invincibility. One terrified Makkan Sharif

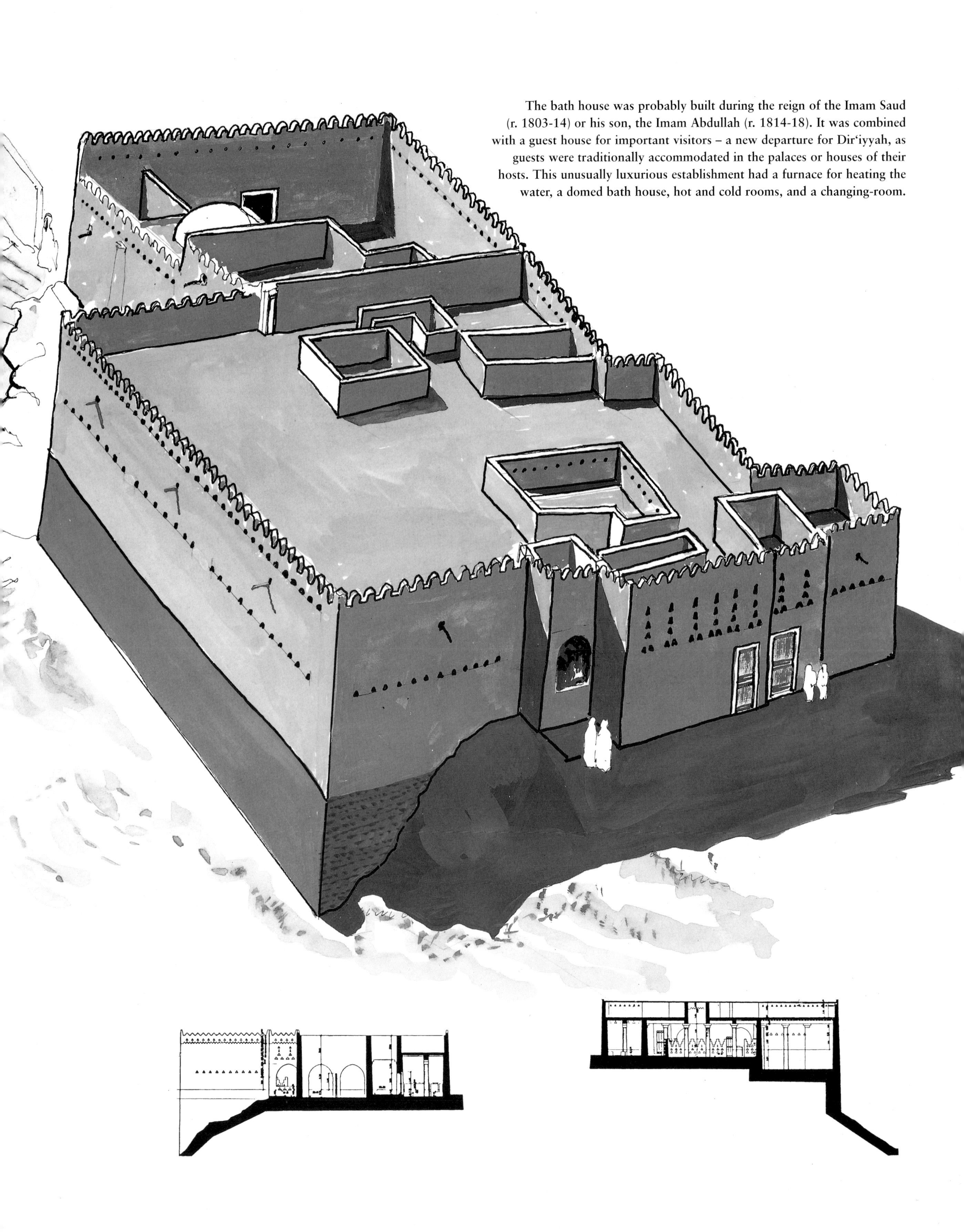

The bath house was probably built during the reign of the Imam Saud (r. 1803-14) or his son, the Imam Abdullah (r. 1814-18). It was combined with a guest house for important visitors – a new departure for Dir'iyyah, as guests were traditionally accommodated in the palaces or houses of their hosts. This unusually luxurious establishment had a furnace for heating the water, a domed bath house, hot and cold rooms, and a changing-room.

Street scene in front of the Palace of Sa'd.

once reported to Ghalib that the Wahhabis "come on like locusts or streams out of the hills after rain."

Fire-power increased during the period of the First Saudi State, through large-scale capture of weapons from its enemies. Matchlocks became commonplace, though they never actually replaced the sabres, lances and spears of the early days. We have Burckhardt's word for it that the Najdi matchlockmen were expert marksmen, and that they could always defeat the enemy in rocky areas by the mere fire of their musketry, although they were often defeated wherever the Turco-Egyptian cavalry had room to act. Lead shot was manufactured locally, as was gunpowder, from saltpetre. The Imam Saud possessed sixty cannon, and there were said to have been eighty at the defence of Dir'iyyah in 1818. However, cannon were singularly ineffective in assault, as mud defences tended to absorb the impact without collapsing, as was shown at Qunfudhah and Rass. Coats of mail were still worn by important leaders. Saud the Great was reputed to wear one in battle. When the demolition of Dir'iyyah began under Ibrahim Pasha in 1818, it is said that eighty coats of mail were found hidden in the walls.

Being a citizen militia, the Saudi forces were essentially temporary, disbanding on completion of the campaign. This made them very effective raiders, but unsuited to permanent occupation and continuing control of an area. However, once a district had been subdued, a governor and a *qadi* were appointed from Dir'iyyah. This, combined with the threat of punitive chastisement from Dir'iyyah, was normally sufficient to ensure adherence to the reform movement. The governor's chief roles were to assist the tax-gatherers, recruit troops and execute the judgments of the *qadi*. Nonetheless, standing garrisons would be placed at strategic points, such as Madinah and Buraymi, or in places where the local people could not be relied upon, and a permanent occupation might ensue. In such cases the system of temporary campaign service had to be modified, and levies might be made to serve continuously for a year or more.

The great battlemented ramparts of Turayf and the oasis of Dir'iyyah as a whole provided effective defence until Ibrahim Pasha's Turco-Egyptian artillery arrived on the scene in 1818. This artillery was able not only to breach fortifications but also to bombard buildings within the walls: Ibn Bishr records intensive bombardments "falling like rain". The Egyptian artillery was more effective than the eighty or so cannon at Dir'iyyah's disposal during the siege.

There were many horses at Dir'iyyah. Most belonged to the royal stud and were lent to cavalrymen on campaign. But many of the well-to-do prided themselves on keeping a horse, despite the extra military obligation it entailed.

At its zenith under the Imam Saud, Dir'iyyah's empire in Arabia was divided into the provinces of al-'Arid, al-Hasa, al-Qasim, Jabal Shammar, al-Haramayn (Makkah and al-Madinah), the Hijaz (south of Taif), and Yemen (the lowland coastal Tihamah: the highlands remained independent).

One of the major social and economic changes under the reform movement was in taxation. The new dispensation demanded that previous taxation practices be replaced by the Islamic alms tax, or *zakah*. As we have seen in the case of Muhammad ibn Saud, this demand was a major cause of resistance among traditional rulers to the adoption of reform. The effectiveness of the new state's writ can be judged from the efficiency with which its tax-collecting was organised and the comprehensiveness of its coverage of both nomads and settlers. This is demonstrated by Ibn Bishr's description of tax-collecting from the nomadic tribes – by all accounts a new experience for them.

Under the Second Saudi State (1824-91), *zakah* on the bedouin was levied at a rate of one camel in 40, one sheep in 100 and one horse in 20, and there is no reason to suppose that these rates did not apply also during the First Saudi State. We are told that the *zakah* from the bedouin went into the Imam Saud's private treasury, where it was used to pay the expenses of his establishment and bodyguard.

From the settled communities *zakah* was levied on agricultural produce which could be measured and stored: that is, grains and some fruits, notably dates. The rate varied: it was at ten per cent on produce from unirrigated land, and five per cent from irrigated plots. There was a ten per cent tax on honey, and a wealth tax on gold and silver of two-and-a-half per cent. Merchants were taxed at the rate of two-and-a-half per cent on the value of goods traded. *Zakah* from the settled communities went in the Bayt al-Mal, or public treasury. The revenue of a district used to be assessed, under the Second Saudi State, about a month before the date harvest by a *wakil* or representative, usually a local man - often a merchant - who visited the plantations inspecting them in the company of a party of camel-riders from the capital. Presumably this is how it was organised under the First Saudi State too.

In time of war, a special additional tax was levied. However, a large part of state revenues during the expansionist years derived from booty. The state was entitled to one-fifth of all plunder taken in battle, while the remaining four-fifths were distributed among the troops. Given the scale of its military successes, quite apart from isolated windfalls such as the plundering of Karbala and the stripping of the Prophet's Tomb in Madinah, this must have been an important factor in the prosperity of Dir'iyyah.

Burckhardt also records an important further source of state revenue, which seems to have been a modification of the previous customary rights of the *ru'asa'*: there was a large public land-holding which had come to the state through conquest. A settlement would be plundered for a first misdemeanour; but for a second offence all property and land would be expropriated to the Bayt al-Mal. Some would then be given to new owners, but most would be left in the hands of its former owners, who would now be lease-holders paying one-third or half of the produce to the Bayt al-Mal. Other state revenues included fines levied for law-breaking, import duties, and the fee charged to pilgrims in return for which the government guaranteed their security. There was also the tribute paid by states which acknowledged Dir'iyyah but did not form part of its domains, such as Bahrain and Muscat. Finally, there was the income from the Imam's personal domains.

Revenues in money and kind from the settled population were gathered first into the local Bayt al-Mal. From here one quarter was assigned to the relief of the poor, paying the *'ulama'* and other clerics and officials of the central government, and public welfare projects such as the repair of mosques and digging of public wells. Half went on the provisioning of soldiers who could not provide for themselves, and on the entertainment of guests. The remainder, usually amounting to a quarter, was sent to the Bayt al-Mal at Dir'iyyah, sometimes in kind but generally in the form of money after a sale of the remaining taxes in kind. Here they were expended similarly, and as alms.

The re-distribution of alms was central to the concept of the just Unitarian ruler – a father-figure who, while seeing to the even-handed enforcement of God's law, also provided for the welfare of all his people. As his Chief Steward was to say of Ibn Saud over a century later, "Every king in the world is supported by his people; but the people of Najd are supported by their king."

The west gate of Turayf led into the part of the town where the poorer families lived – though, unlike elsewhere in Najd, their houses were built of rough stone plastered with mud.

The inside of the mosque of Subalat Mudi. This mosque also has a semi-basement prayer-hall directly beneath.

Above: The Dir'iyyah fortification wall protects the left bank of Wadi Hanifah atop the cliff of Qurayn, towards the southern end of the oasis.

Right: The bed of Wadi Hanifah in flood below the working well just outside Turayf.

Above: The farmland on each side of Wadi Hanifah was protected from the floodwaters by solid revetments of stone blocks, like this modern one opposite Turayf

Below: The Turayf bluff juts out to a bend in Wadi Hanifah, with the cliff of Qurayn in the background.

INTERLUDE

A French Agent in Dir'iyyah?

Fathallah Sayigh's mysterious travels

An intriguing contemporary report found its way into European consciousness when it was published in French in 1835 as Volume IV of the poet Lamartine's *Voyage en Orient*. This was a translation from Arabic into French of the memoirs of a Syrian agent of Napoleon I, one Fathallah Sayigh, a Maronite Christian from Aleppo, who accompanied a French agent, the Provençal nobleman Lascaris de Ventimille. Of Lascaris's presence in the area there is no doubt, for he is recorded in the papers of the French embassy in Cairo, where he was to die in 1817.

Sayigh claimed that he and Lascaris travelled in the Syrian desert and Persia between 1810 and 1814, trying with some success to create a grand alliance of the bedouin tribes against the Ottomans and, ultimately, the British, as part of the French design to sever Britain's communications with her eastern possessions – a mission similar to the one Palgrave was to claim for himself fifty years later. Their chosen instrument was Duray'i Ibn Sha'lan, paramount shaykh of the Ruwala. The final episode in their adventure was a visit Sayigh claimed that he made to Dir'iyyah to harness the Saudis to their cause, and Sayigh describes long interviews with Abdullah ibn Saud as well as the town of Dir'iyyah itself.

The translation published by Lamartine was scattered with errors and was generally dismissed by Arabists. There are indeed many problems surrounding the authenticity of Sayigh's report, even whether he made the trip at all and, if he did, the date of his visit. A new translation has recently been published by the French scholar Joseph Chelhod, who argues strongly for the basic reliability of Sayigh's account. What Sayigh has to say is of great interest, and deserves a place here.

Fathallah Sayigh claimed to have visited Dir'iyyah accompanied by Duray'i, the Ruwala chieftain – an historical character who is attested in Burckhardt's work as chief of the Ruwala when, as allies of Saud the Great, they joined the raids into the Hawran and Syria in 1810. The date of Sayigh's visit is nowhere stated, though Chelhod concludes that 1813 is most likely. On the route through Najd Sayigh noted that, while Jabal Shammar and Najd were under Wahhabi rule and rite, this was through fear rather than choice.

It was a brave decision to make the journey to Dir'iyyah, because the Ruwala and their allies had recently inflicted a defeat on a Saudi raiding party (at the so-called Battle of Hama which, if it occurred, may have taken place in 1812). So they were prepared for a hostile reception by the Saudi ruler, which in the event is what they received.

Sayigh gives a lengthy description of Dir'iyyah. It is clear that what he is describing is in fact the main settlement of Turayf:

> After fourteen days of travel since we left our own people, we reached the palm groves of Dir'iyyah. We marched for four hours through the palms, which touched each other to form a sort of barrier against the enemy. Having traversed this forest, we arrived at the entrance to the town. It was surrounded by little black hillocks of date stones accumulated over the years. With time and the pressure of settling one on another, the date stones had come to form a kind of wall or barrier protecting the town where we made our entrance. Built on the side of a wadi, the town has gates which are opened in the morning and closed in the evening. We continued our march up to the palace, where we were received. This palace, very large and of two storeys, is built of stones.
>
> Ibn Saud, once informed of Duray'i's arrival, had us lodged in a clean and well-furnished apartment in the palace. A meal was brought in for us straight away. At the beginning of the afternoon, Duray'i requested permission to present himself to Ibn Saud. He was informed that he could present himself without first seeking an audience, this formality not being customary at the Wahhabi court. We entered the *majlis* where Ibn Saud, surrounded by the notables of his court, received his guests. We greeted him, one by one, without taking his hand or kissing the flaps of his robe in the Ottoman manner. On entering the room, each of us made a gesture of the hand and said: "Peace be upon you, o Ibn Saud", and took a seat. Only the slaves remained standing. Before us we saw a man sitting in the middle of the couch, about forty-five years old, with a black beard. He wore a robe (*qumbaz*) of white cotton, fastened with a waist-band of equally white muslin. Over his shoulder was a black cloak (*mashlah*) without embroidery (from al-Hasa). On his head he wore a *kufiyyah* and a turban of red and white striped cotton called a *dasman*, and he held in his hand sticks of a tree called *mahlab*. He dressed like this all the year round, having forbidden the wearing, in his dominions, of silk and luxurious brightly coloured clothing. As for the audience chamber where he held counsel, it was furnished simply with matting, woollen rugs and cushions upholstered in wool and made in the Yemen.

The audience began with an icy silence. "Ibn Saud" then gave vent to his resentment against Duray'i and the Ruwala, and the guests were confined without food to their quarters, where they had plenty of time to ponder the prudence of their enterprise. After three days Ibn Saud relented and listened to what Sayigh and Duray'i had to propose: an anti-Ottoman alliance of the Arab tribes. The atmosphere lightened, and they were allowed the freedom of Dir'iyyah, which Sayigh describes as follows:

> The next day, we took a walk in Dir'iyyah. It is a small town, well watered, and built of pale-coloured stone. Its seven thousand inhabitants are almost all relatives, confidants, advisers, commanders, generals and clients of the Wahhabi. There is no food market there, as everyone lives off his own produce. As for visitors, they are accommodated in the houses of the people, who are very hospitable. Various different crafts are practised, notably the weaving of cotton cloth, headcloths and red-and-white striped waist-bands. They also make black and white cloaks. Armourers, farriers, saddlers and felt-makers all have workshops, and felt is manufactured in large quantities.
>
> The people of Dir'iyyah have little taste for hard work. They like repose, ease and the sweet life. They are fond of meeting their friends and taking a long time to say very little, just for the pleasure of chatting and passing the time. Their women are not very beautiful, most of them being very dark-skinned, to the extent that they regard someone as fair-skinned whom we would describe as swarthy. When they go out they drape themselves in a capacious black cloak, large enough for two. They go bare-foot, without sandals, like the bedouin of the desert, from whom they differ only in wearing a veil. Their clothes are just like their desert sisters', but they do not wear silk, which is forbidden here. However, their headbands like their waistcoats are threaded with gold.
>
> The gardens, situated in a valley [*i.e. Wadi Hanifah and tributaries*] near the town, produce very fine fruits: bananas, figs, pomegranates, dates, lemons, oranges, sugar cane, melons, courgettes, coconuts. The district also produces wheat, which is carefully irrigated, yellow and white corn [*presumably millet*], from which they make a flour for bread-making, but which is also used to make other dishes. The people keep a great number of chickens, as well as horses and flocks. They eat camel-meat and camel's milk, but mutton is rarely consumed. They eat modestly: a mere morsel satisfies them. Their expenditure is also very limited, as everyone lives off the produce of his own gardens. Again, they dress very modestly, not being given to wasteful expense any more with their clothes than with their food. Besides, at Dir'iyyah everything is cheap, and there are few things which entail any expense. Things which are lacking there are imported, by boat, from Yanbu' to Mukha, in the Yemen, where coffee is produced. ... Mukha is a large town, in the sphere of influence of Sana'ah, near the Jawf, six days distance from the Bab al-Mandab. It is part of the Yemen, but these days is in the Wahhabi dominions. It is a considerable town, as important as Aleppo. Its people pay the tithe to Ibn Saud, whom they deeply dread. So, the people of Mukha come to Dir'iyyah with everything that that city lacks. They sell their merchandise there and buy, in exchange, sheep, horses, cloaks (*mashlah*), waistcoats, felt and plenty of other products. The market, the only place of trade in this town, is held every Wednesday. But the people of Dir'iyyah also sell their merchandise in the Hadramawt. That region is today almost in ruins, although it was formerly thriving. Some of the settlements there, despite their poverty, pay the tithe to the Wahhabi, who coerces them.
>
> Coinage of various different countries is in circulation at Dir'iyyah: the thaler [*probably the Maria Theresa dollar*], the gold piece known as *mashkhass*, the Hungarian gold piece, the half- and quarter-thaler, the old milled Egyptian gold piece, the old gold piece stamped with a rose known as *Abu Wardah*, and coinage of small denominations. However, Turkish currency is not legal tender.

Sayigh goes on to describe in great detail an interview he had with "Ibn Saud" about Christianity, aspects of government including the appointment of governors and the collection of taxes, and meetings with the Wahhabi generals Abdullah al-Haddal and Abu Nuqtah. He and Duray'i finally succeeded in concluding an alliance with Dir'iyyah, and left for the north on the best of terms.

Sayigh's story raises doubts strikingly similar to those surrounding Palgrave's visit to Riyadh in 1862. Like Palgrave's, his story was probably written well after the events he describes, allowing plenty of scope for inaccuracies. Even granted that he and Lascaris

The palaces of Salwa from Wadi Hanifah. The remains of the Salwa wall can be seen in front, pierced by a large gateway with a bastion to each side.

were entrusted by the French with the mission to unite the tribes, did they really achieve the successes he claims? Did he exaggerate their achievements and journeys after the event, knowing that nobody would be able to check up on them? A short account of an earlier journey they claimed to have made across Persia to the Indian frontier with the Ruwala does seem to be invention; was the journey to Dir'iyyah similarly invented? The enterprise was abandoned on Sayigh's return with Lascaris to Istanbul, perhaps in 1814, because Napoleon's defeat in Russia in November 1812 meant that wider French ambitions had to be relinquished. There is no way of checking Sayigh's story from external sources, and so we have to look at what might be taken as discrepancies in his account itself to try to determine its reliability.

First of all, the forty-five-year-old "Ibn Saud" he decribes meeting cannot be the Imam Saud, who reigned until his death at sixty-eight in 1814. He must have been Saud's son Abdullah, and in fact Sayigh actually refers to him as the ruler Abdullah once in his report. However, this is not necessarily a problem: Sayigh nowhere calls his Ibn Saud the Imam, and Saud might have been out of Dir'iyyah at the time. It was not uncommon for the heir apparent to take charge of affairs – Palgrave never got to meet the Imam Faisal in 1862, dealing instead with his son Abdullah. The description of Ibn Saud's palace as two-storeyed, as Abdullah's may have been, rather than four-storeyed, as were the Salwa Palaces of Saud, could be taken to be an authentic detail which confirms Sayigh's story.

Other problems raise stronger suspicions. Sayigh claims to have dined with the Asiri chieftain Abu Nuqtah. Abu Nuqtah died in 1809 and was succeeded by Shaykh Tamy of the Rufaydah. It is odd to say of any Arab society that mutton was rarely consumed (especially in the light of Reinaud's report to the contrary). Like Corancez, he describes Dir'iyyah as being built of stone. The buildings were indeed often raised on a foundation of cut, pale-coloured local stone which was continued for several courses above ground level, but one could scarcely call it a stone-built town unless one resolutely confined one's gaze to eye-level and below. Although much of Dir'iyyah was indeed built of stone, unusually for a Najdi town, especially its western quarter, the stone was hidden beneath a layer of mud plaster. It is just possible that Sayigh saw stones beneath the mud plaster and assumed that the walls were constructed of a core of stone to full height. On the other hand, it is tempting to accuse him of copying Corancez' hearsay description of Dir'iyyah, which was published in 1810.

Another jarring note is struck by the date of his departure from Dir'iyyah. As they left, he says, a messenger arrived announcing the setting forth of Muhammad Ali's forces from Yanbu' to Madinah. This is usually taken to mean the first Egyptian departure from Yanbu', in January 1812. However, the context makes it clear that it cannot have been the first attempt upon Madinah. The second attempt was made in October-November 1812 – not so long before Sayigh's spring visit to Dir'iyyah, if it was made in 1813, but still a long time for the news to reach Dir'iyyah. Alternatively, the reference could be to the arrival of Ibrahim Pasha's expedition in 1816 – but then this would be too late to accord with their arrival in Aleppo and Istanbul to the news of Napoleon's Russian campaign in 1812.

Finally, could Sayigh have gleaned his information about Dir'iyyah from other sources? Lascaris apparently met "an English explorer Shaikh Ibrahim" in early 1812. Since this was the name he travelled under, this can be none other than Burckhardt. Lascaris also knew Lady Hester Stanhope, the eccentric English "Queen of the Desert" who had made her home amongst the Arabs of Syria and whose bedouin contacts were excellent, and he had close contacts with well-informed French officials in Damascus, Cairo and Baghdad. Corancez, for example, was a French official in Damascus, where he wrote his account of the Wahhabis. There was no shortage of possible informants and, by the time that Sayigh came to write the account of his alleged trip to Dir'iyyah, he may also have had access to published information about central Arabia by Ali Bey, Jomard and Mengin as well as Burckhardt.

So, the answer must be that, by the time he came to write his account, Sayigh could have compiled his information on Dir'iyyah from various sources. While it is almost certain that he did join Lascaris in undertaking a mission among the bedouin on behalf of the French, one cannot avoid the suspicion that, like Palgrave's, his story contains exaggerations and is occasionally embellished with sheer invention. Whether or not the journey to Dir'iyyah belongs in the latter category must, for now, remain an intriguing mystery which awaits a solution.

CHAPTER SEVEN

Invasion, Siege and Surrender

The Ottomans strike back

TUSUN'S CAMPAIGN INTO AL-QASIM, 1815

With the accession in 1814 of the Imam Abdullah ibn Saud, the tide of war had begun to turn in favour of the Egyptians. As we have seen at the end of Chapter 5, the Imam's brother, the handsome and charismatic Faisal, had suffered the crushing defeat at Bisal in 1815 which finally dispelled the myth of Wahhabi invincibility. Imam Abdullah believed, rightly, that a Turco-Egyptian invasion of Najd from the north, via al-Qasim, would soon follow, and he gathered his forces there in expectation.

Tusun, who had been appointed governor of Madinah by his father Muhammad Ali, was indeed anxious following Bisal to press into Najd. Without waiting for his father's permission, Tusun left his valiant lieutenant Thomas Keith, a Scot who had adopted Islam and was now known as Ibrahim Agha, in charge of Madinah, and advanced on Hanakiyyah. Muhammad Ali had meanwhile arrived in Madinah, only to be obliged to return to Egypt to deal with domestic unrest. Tusun ignored his father's attempts to call him back and advanced into al-Qasim, seizing Rass with a surprise night assault. The bedouin, notably the Harb and Mutayr, always quick to acknowledge a victor, flocked to his side.

The Imam Abdullah, already dismayed by the reverse at Bisal, must have been further alarmed by this loss of support. The truth is that Tusun was in a weak position: his resources were slender and his supply line had been cut behind him when Thomas Keith and a detachment of horse were wiped out at Mu'awiyah near Hanakiyyah. Keith was regarded, even by the Imam Abdullah himself, as the bravest man in Tusun's army. Added to this, the bedouin's flocks were devouring all the fodder in Rass, which would soon have made a hazardous advance necessary.

The Imam failed to take advantage of this and meekly sought a truce, which Muhammad Ali was encouraging Tusun to make, allowing both sides to withdraw. Its provisional terms were that Dir'iyyah should renounce its claims to the Holy Cities, that the Imam should acknowledge the suzerainty of the Ottoman Sultan, submit to the authority of the governor of Madinah, return the treasures taken from the Tomb of the Prophet, and allow the passage of pilgrim caravans through his territory. The Egyptians in their turn would agree not to invade Najd. Envoys were sent to Muhammad Ali in Cairo to conclude it.

On the face of it, this arrangement should have satisfied both parties: Muhammad Ali would have ensured the security of the Holy Cities for the Ottoman Sultan, and Najd would have been safe from invasion. But the Imam reckoned without the wily Albanian's growing ambition to create an Egyptian empire in Arabia, Palestine and Syria – which he was to pursue until 1840. Moreover, Muhammad Ali had always promised the Sultan that he would destroy Dir'iyyah. The hapless envoys returned from Cairo with Muhammad Ali's insistence on the Imam's formal submission including the ceding not only of Dir'iyyah to Madinah but also, unexpectedly, of the province of al-Hasa. He must have known the Imam would reject such terms, and would thus provide him with a pretext for a full-scale invasion of Najd, the stated aim of which would be the destruction of Dir'iyyah.

Brydges reproduced this contemporary engraving of the captive Imam Abdullah ibn Saud in 1818 in his *Brief History of the Wahauby*.

IBRAHIM PASHA'S CAMPAIGN INTO NAJD, 1816-1818

Having indeed rejected Muhammad Ali's demand for submission, the Imam assembled his chiefs. The call to arms went out in mosques throughout Najd. Provisions were collected, and thirty thousand fighting men were brought together under the leadership of the Imam himself and his brother Faisal.

For a Najdi ruler, the Imam Abdullah had unprecedented resources at his command. Some said that no Arabian prince had attained such magnificence since the days of the Umayyad Caliphs. His bodyguard numbering several hundred men, together with two thousand horses, innumerable camels, and the spoils of decades of successful campaigns were instantly at his disposal. Tens of thousands of fighters could be levied at short notice. Dir'iyyah itself was prosperous and well-defended, with a population, it is thought, grown to around thirty thousand people including women and children – more than Riyadh in the 1920s. His recent wedding celebrations had required the slaughter of 350 camels and 1500 sheep. Every day five hundred people were entertained at his expense, as under his father Saud. His own personal qualities were renowned. He was said to have galloped his mare at the age of five. He had been groomed for the leadership of the community of God by his father Saud, participating in all his counsels. His valour was proven in battle, and he made it a rule to lead his troops in person. He was a poet. His generosity, piety and deep knowledge of the Qur'an were all up to the high standards expected of the Imam of the *muwahhidun*.

And yet there is no denying that he lacked his father's flair in the field. An over-cautious

Muhammad Ali, ruler of Egypt and father of Ibrahim Pasha and Tusun Pasha, in an engraving published by Driault in *La formation de l'empire de Mohamed Aly de l'Araby au Soudain 1814-1823.*

commander, he overlooked opportunities for harrassing the enemy on his own ground. A reason for this may have been that by now Dir'iyyah's hold over the tribes and towns was somewhat less than in the heyday of the reform movement. Ibn Bishr's opinion of him was that though he was a brave man, he lacked political acumen. There was dissatisfaction in Najd. Though loyalty could be bought by the prospect of material success in campaigns, tribe and town were less inspired than formerly by the sense of divine mission. Ibn Bishr's history hints that the Imam Saud's splendour compared unfavourably with his father 'Abd al-'Aziz's simplicity, and that the taste for luxury, (in Saud's case accompanied by a self-confessed avarice), perhaps undercut Dir'iyyah's ideological credibility. The Imam's campaigns in al-Qasim during 1815-16 aimed specifically at bringing disaffected elements into line: he destroyed the walls of Khabra and Bukayriyyah, took hostages from Rass, and marched in pursuit of the bedouin tribes of Harb and Mutayr who had sided with the Egyptians.

On 23rd September 1816, after months of preparation, Muhammad Ali's campaign force disembarked at Yanbu'. It consisted of ten thousand men – perhaps a quarter of all the troops available in Egypt – including three thousand North African cavalrymen able to cope with the rigours of the Najdi summer. There were North African, Turkish and Albanian infantrymen and a dozen or so artillery pieces complete with gunners and artificers. The force was under the command of Tusun's elder brother Ibrahim. Though a man of only twenty-five, Ibrahim was to prove a determined and ruthless leader.

The campaign was given the superficial character of a holy war against heresy. Ibrahim was to deposit a gift at the Tomb of the Prophet at Madinah, and took an oath not to cut his hair until victory had been achieved. After reaching Madinah and Hanakiyyah, he was promoted by Sultan Mahmoud to a Pasha of Three Tails, and was thus confirmed as official representative of the Commander of the Faithful. This did not deter Ibrahim, however, from availing himself of infidel expertise, for his force was accompanied by at least five Europeans. These included his personal physician Antonio Scoto and three other Italian doctors, Gentili, Todeschini and Socio. But the most important foreigner was a siege engineer named Vaissière, one of the many French soldiers who had left home to seek their fortune after Napoleon's defeat at Waterloo.

With Ibrahim's arrival the stage was set. Never in history had central Arabia submitted to foreign invasion. What ensued was an epic struggle worthy of Homer's Greeks and Trojans in the Iliad. Against the political and religious background of the conflict, a tale unfolds of rivalry between two powerful personalities, a saga of honour, ambition and pitiful shame; of triumph, despair and bitter humiliation. For the people of Dir'iyyah the workings of divine providence must have seemed increasingly unfathomable. The Egyptian soldiery must have felt as much at the mercy of their leaders as of the enemy. Moments of heroic resilience in grievous hardship are conjured out of brutality, bad faith and catastrophe. The Imam Abdullah emerges as a tragic figure who, despite his many virtues and his territorial advantages, was not to be spared the fatal consequences of one flawed strand in his own personality.

In the winter of 1816-17 Ibrahim marched east from Madinah, where he had collected an able cavalry commander, 'Awzun Ali, and made a base at Hanakiyyah. Here his successes against the tribes persuaded many to throw in their lot with him. He awaited reinforcements from Egypt. Meanwhile the Imam Abdullah moved into al-Qasim. At first simply planning to rely on harrassment and to wait until Ibrahim's supplies ran low, he later conceived the more imaginative strategy of sweeping round Ibrahim, seizing Madinah,

Ibrahim Pasha, the conqueror of Dir'iyyah, as portrayed in *Rambles in Egypt and Candia* by C. Rochfort Scott, 1837.

and then, with the enemy cut off from the Hijaz, falling on him from behind. His brother Faisal was sent south to take first Makkah and then Jeddah and Yanbu', thus to ensure the Turco-Egyptian army's complete isolation.

However, the plan faltered. At about the same time a second force, of ten thousand men under Hasan Pasha, arrived from Egypt to garrison Makkah against the Wahhabis. Eventually it was to be sent to invade Yemen, as part of Muhammad Ali's wider imperial ambitions.

Next, the Imam rashly decided to take on a detachment of Ibrahim Pasha's troops which had taken the wells of Mu'awiyah. The odds seemed stacked in favour of Abdullah's ten thousand camel-riders, as they fell upon 'Awzun Ali's four hundred cavalry, one thousand infantry, some bedouin warriors and a single field piece. But Abdullah's men suffered a humiliating defeat. When Sadleir passed this spot in 1819, the ground was still strewn with skeletons, a further poignant reminder of Saud the Great's advice never to engage the Egyptians in the open plain.

When other skirmishes at Hanakiyyah went against the Imam, he decided instead to fall back into al-Qasim to protect the approach to southern Najd. He ravaged the country as he went, but this only served to persuade more tribes to go over to Ibrahim. In May the Pasha, covered by his alliance with the Harb and Mutayr, made the arduous advance on Rass and its six thousand inhabitants confident that, like Tusun in 1815, he could take it immediately.

In the event Rass proved a major setback for Ibrahim. His first assault was hasty and badly planned, the defenders killing hundreds of Ibrahim's hapless soldiery, who were in any case shot by their own commanders if they tried to retreat. The town's heroic defenders, according to Sadleir, showed more science than the Turkish general. They repulsed four major assaults. Ibrahim's cannonballs simply buried themselves ineffectively in the mud walls. As the siege wore on in the summer heat, the morale of Ibrahim's men was further eroded by the usual desert discomforts – high winds and dust storms. They succumbed to disease. Faisal's men came up and harrassed their supply lines. However, these were kept open by the Pasha's tribal allies. The inefficiency of the besiegers allowed at least two supply caravans to enter Rass unimpeded. Estimates of total Egyptian losses during the three-and-a-half month siege vary from six hundred to some 3400 men and a vast amount of ammunition. The defenders lost only 160 men. Whichever figure one accepts for Egyptian losses, the siege of Rass dealt a serious blow to their campaign plans.

The lengthening siege afforded the Imam Abdullah another chance to seize the initiative. Once again he failed to take it. His distrust of the leaders of Rass may explain his failure to come to their support. Instead, as in 1815, he offered peace if Ibrahim would lift the siege. Ibrahim responded by demanding that Rass be delivered into his hands, to which its governor boldly retorted "Come and take it then!"

Negotiations dragged on fruitlessly. Abdullah and Faisal withdrew deeper into Najd, abandoning the strategy of harrassment. Effectively they left al-Qasim to its fate. Ibrahim and the chiefs of Rass reached a curious arrangement by which the Egyptians were to abandon the siege, take what provisions the people of Rass were prepared to sell them, and move on to 'Unayzah; if 'Unayzah fell, then Rass would accept an Egyptian garrison; if 'Unayzah held out, Rass would continue to be treated as an enemy.

By-passing Khabra, which was included in the agreement with Rass, Ibrahim set about besieging 'Unayzah, the flourishing commercial centre of al-Qasim with a population of eight thousand people. At this point he was joined by reinforcements: another able cavalry commander, Rishwan Agha, with a detachment of horse. 'Unayzah's great fortress of Qasr al-Safa, with its five-metre-thick walls, seemed impregnable. Up till now, it seems, Vaissière's advice had gone unheeded, but

The Ottoman Empire in 1800

EUROPE
RUSSIA
MOLDAVIA
WALLACHIA
BOSNIA
Belgrade
Sarajevo
Danube
BLACK SEA
CASPIAN SEA
GEORGIA
Edirne
RUMELIA
Salonica
Istanbul
ARMENIA
ASIA
Ankara
ANATOLIA
Izmir
Athens
Konya
Tunis
Tigris
Aleppo
Mosul
TUNISIA
MEDITERRANEAN SEA
CRETE
SYRIA
IRAN
Beirut
Damascus
Euphrates
Baghdad
Tripolis
TRIPOLITANIA
Alexandria
Jerusalem
Basra
Cairo
KUWAIT
AL-HASA
GULF
FEZZAN
EGYPT
Qatif
NAJD
Hofuf
Sharjah
Al-Madinah
Dir'iyyah
OMAN
Yanbu'
HIJAZ
Nile
Jeddah
Makkah
AFRICA
RED SEA
ASIR
0 km 700
N
San'a
YEMEN
HADRAMAWT
ARABIAN SEA
Mukha
Aden
Ottoman Empire, 1800
Saudi Influence, 1808

Ibrahim, dreading further losses before 'Unayzah, now entrusted the direction of the siege to him. The town surrendered after only six days, when a lucky shot ignited the powder magazine in the fort, making a large breach in the wall. From then on Ibrahim kept the Frenchman constantly by his side.

Rass duly let in an Egyptian garrison. Buraydah, in those days only half the size of 'Unayzah, succumbed to a four-day bombardment. Ibrahim was now master of al-Qasim with its plentiful food supplies. Abdullah and Faisal had withdrawn to Shaqra, the chief town of al-Washm, half way to Dir'iyyah. Ibrahim planned to use al-Qasim as his base, and he spent three months at Buraydah consolidating his position there while further reinforcements arrived from Egypt.

At Shaqra the Imam Abdullah gave orders to fortify Dir'iyyah. It is probably to this time that much of the elaborate system of walls and towers along each side of Wadi Hanifah owe their completion. He trusted to the long march south through the Najdi heartland to exhaust the invader. Even if Ibrahim were to reach Dir'iyyah, the town's defences would frustrate him. Isolated, the besiegers would succumb to fatigue, hunger and disease. Like the Tsar of Russia's Generals Janvier and Février in 1812, the Najdi summer months would be his best generals. However, he reckoned without Ibrahim's resilience and indomitable spirit, which evoked comparison with Bonaparte himself.

A Wahhabi bedouin soldier *(left)* with an "Azami" tribesman, as depicted in a lithograph after E. Prisse d'Avennes in J.A. St. John's *Oriental Album,* 1848.

Below: **Sultan Mahmoud II, the Ottoman Caliph who ruled the empire from 1808 until 1839. From Thomas Allom's *Character and Costume in Turkey and Italy*, c.1838.**

In January 1818 Ibrahim set out from al-Qasim with 4500 men, 6000 baggage camels, and artillery pieces which kept getting stuck in the sand. It was an arduous march, and one which he would have been unable to make without extensive support from the bedouin tribes, chief among whom were the Mutayr under their chief Faisal al-Dawish, to whom Ibrahim had pledged the governorship of Dir'iyyah once captured. Many villages en route had been abandoned and stripped of supplies. Mudhnib, Ushayqir and Fara'ah in turn offered submission at Ibrahim's appearance before their gates.

The siege of Shaqra was a brief affair. Vaissière's advice was once again sought. Shaqra was well prepared for a siege, with a moat and plentiful supplies laid in. But a breach was opened in the plantation circuit wall, savage fighting took place within the gardens and, leaving more than a hundred dead, the defenders retired inside the town. The town itself was then tightly invested and bombarded. After only eight days Shaqra's leaders were suing for peace. Like 'Unayzah's, Shaqra's seemed a feeble resistance after Rass. Shaqra's governor Hamad ibn Yahya ibn Ghayhab was a brother-in-law of the Imam Abdullah, but it was a prosperous, non-fanatical place conducting brisk business with Iraq and Syria, and its loyalty to the reform movement was probably fragile. An expansive and stylish Najdi town, its population estimated at some six thousand, its walls and

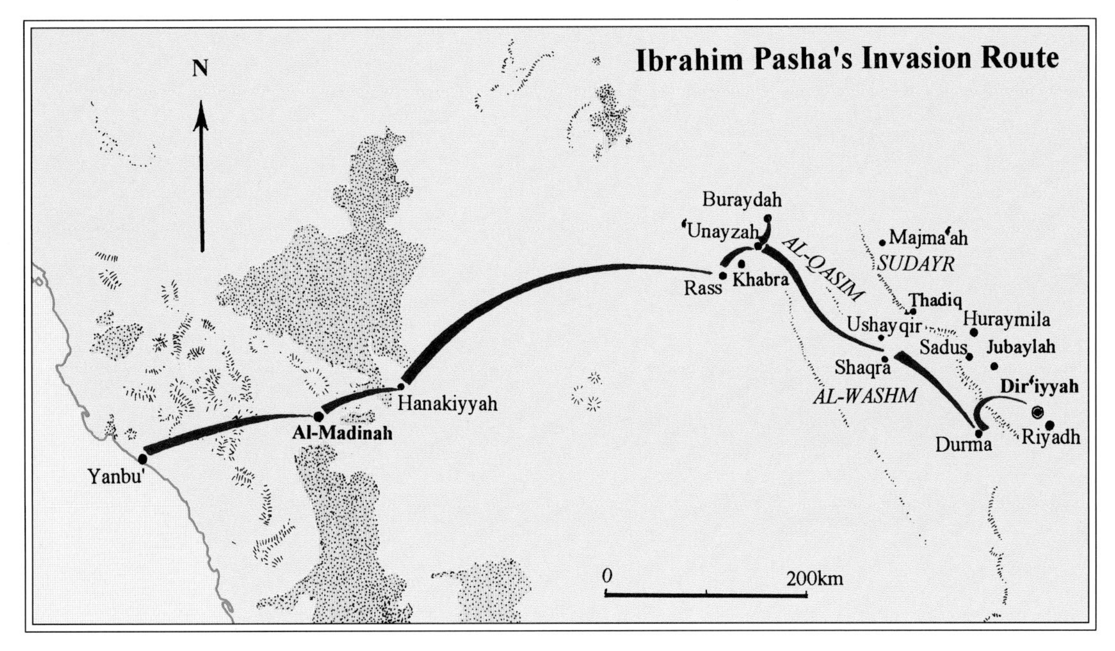

old town can still be seen today. Ibrahim disarmed its fourteen hundred fighting men and sent them away on condition that they took no further part in the war. That done he felt confident enough to establish a forward base there, complete with a field hospital run by Gentili. Shaqra contained sufficient supplies to provision his army for a month, and weapons and powder to distribute among his Najdi allies. Rishwan Agha was sent off to receive the submission of the towns of Sudayr.

After two weeks at Shaqra the invading force moved on towards Durma. As gruesome proof of his successes Ibrahim sent home to Cairo twelve hundred pairs of ears cut from enemy dead. His soldiers were well rewarded for each pair of ears, and this grisly custom seems to have been one of the main motivating factors in maintaining morale for the fight among his otherwise hard-pressed men.

However, there seem to have been murmurings in Cairo: Hasan Pasha, who had suffered a reverse at the hands of the Imam of Yemen, had had to be reinforced from Egypt. The war in Arabia was a severe drain on Muhammad Ali's resources, and he may have been wondering why Ibrahim was taking so long. Ibrahim kept asking for more troops and equipment to replace his losses. News that he had reached Dir'iyyah would be followed by contradictory reports that he was still reducing yet another small town as he toiled through Najd. There were rumours in Cairo that he was to be replaced by Khalil Pasha.

On 1st March 1818 Ibrahim arrived before Durma, and camped at Muzahimiyyah nearby. Durma was an important settlement, at five thousand people not much smaller than Shaqra. It had been colonised in the 16th century by settlers from Dir'iyyah, and its gardens supplied many foodstuffs to the capital. As a loyal Saudi stronghold, its governor Saud a cousin of the Imam, its resistance could be expected to be fierce, but Ibrahim had been led to believe that it would fall easily. When Durma put up a vigorous defence, he decided on a rapid and brutal assault. Vaissière was sent to reconnoitre for the best place to breach the walls. Two days of concentrated artillery fire did the job, and the troops went in. The slaughter went on for several days: all males over the age of ten were butchered, and blood ran in the corpse-choked streets. It was reported that a thousand men died on the Saudi side to just sixty of the attackers. The usual reward for every pair of ears was granted, Ibrahim himself taking part personally in the killing. Saud ibn Abdullah and his men had taken refuge in the fort, and Ibrahim decided to spare them the usual bombardment because of the horses, weapons and supplies they had with them. He let them go to Dir'iyyah on condition that they took no further part in the war – a false hope, as it was to turn out.

The Imam Abdullah meanwhile was organising the defence of Dir'iyyah. Preparations included converting one of the Salwa Palaces into a large storehouse. Vaissière reported with wonderment that the Saudis did not take advantage of their superior mobility to harrass Ibrahim's troops and disrupt their supply lines. Their horses were excellent, and the toughness of the Wahhabi fighter was famed. Vaissière was amazed that the Pasha's cavalrymen seemed unable to catch an enemy foot-soldier even on the open plain. It would have been easy to follow Saud the Great's advice to avoid direct confrontation, and wear the invader down by continual harrassment. Yet the Imam may have calculated that his loss of tribal support rendered even this course too risky. So he chose to rely on Dir'iyyah's defences and its large population to resist a surely depleted invading force.

This strategy led to yet another lost opportunity. Ibrahim, delayed by a storm, left Durma, according to Sadleir, with 5,600 men, including cavalry and infantry, and twelve artillery pieces. The route to Dir'iyyah – a twelve-hour march – passed up the Tuwayq escarpment via the narrow Haysiyyah defile. How easy at that point for even a few men to cause havoc among the enemy! But the invaders reached 'Uyaynah, which was now just a farming settlement in Wadi Hanifah, without incident. From there Ibrahim marched down the wadi to Jubaylah and Malqa, where he halted.

THE SIEGE OF DIR'IYYAH, MARCH-SEPTEMBER 1818

Ibrahim left the main body of his army at Malqa, and went with eight hundred horsemen and a cannon to reconnoitre a suitable camping ground. At the first northern fortifications of the Dir'iyyah oasis, a skirmish ensued, and he retired to Malqa. Next day he came south again, to 'Ilb (where the dam across Wadi Hanifah stands today), having decided to set up camp there out of reach of the defenders' artillery. The palm gardens of 'Ilb belonged to Faisal ibn Saud. Ibrahim was driven off, but returned two or three days later with his entire force, and set up camp athwart the wadi, preparing defences and building offensive positions from which his artillery could fire on the defenders.

Ibrahim's strategy was necessarily laborious. His force was much too small to contemplate surrounding Dir'iyyah. By this time the entire settlement area of Dir'iyyah was fortified as we see it today, with walls and bastions lining the heights on each side of Wadi Hanifah, from near 'Ilb some eight kilometres southwards to beyond Mulaybid. Turayf itself was enclosed by a secondary wall extending from the main fortification around the bluff on which it stood overlooking Wadi Hanifah. So a conventional siege, cutting off supplies and contact with the outside world, was out of the question. Even the usual method of reducing a Najdi town, by breaching a weak part of the fortifications and sending men in, was a high-risk strategy at Dir'iyyah because of its size, complexity and number of settlements. Instead, Ibrahim's plan was to work his way down the wadi, taking the defences on the heights on each side and occupying strategic points as they fell. He therefore divided his force into three: a central one to advance down the wadi itself, with two wings to reduce the fortifications on either side.

Dir'iyyah's defences were in fact vulnerable at several points. Wherever a tributary entered Wadi Hanifah there was valuable farmland extending up it. The tributary could not be spanned by a wall and culvert as it would either block the flood waters, or else be swept away. The fortification walls therefore stopped short at a tower on the heights on each side. Ibrahim consistently tried to take advantage of these tributary gaps to attack the front-line defenders from the rear.

The Imam Abdullah sent men under his brothers Faisal, Ibrahim and Fahd to confront the Egyptian positions. His northern turrets were manned with cannon, and Faisal and his men dug themselves in within gunshot range of the Egyptians and occupied vantage points. A detachment under Saud ibn Abdullah was sent to the southern end of the oasis, where Wadi Hanifah bends, to guard the heights of Qurayn and Sha'ib Safar. Saud ibn Abdullah thus broke the undertaking he gave to Ibrahim at Durma. The fortifications and turrets on either side of Wadi Hanifah were manned by the less able fighters, who were ordered simply to defend and not come out into the open.

After a period of fierce fighting, Ibrahim's men managed to erect two gun emplacements under cover of night within range of one of the northern towers in the area of the tributary Wadi Ghubayrah. Cavalry under Rishwan Agha were sent to infiltrate behind the defenders once a breach was made. Ibrahim had positioned men to protect the batteries and to block outflanking movements or flight into the desert. The bombardment began and, as soon as a breach was made, the defenders fled into the gardens in the wadi, pursued by the enemy and abandoning their cannon, ammunition, supplies and wounded.

The walls of the oasis of Shaqra *(above)* still survive. Fortifications like this enclosed the entire cultivated area in most Najdi oases. The greenery within contrasted with the aridity outside, as shown at Marat near Shaqra *(right)*.

The reception room *(diwaniyyah)* in a Najdi house usually had a highly decorated coffee hearth, like this relatively recent one *(below)* in an old house in Marat, near Shaqra.

Prisoners were killed on the instant. But the Pasha was unable to follow this up because of shortage of supplies, and chose instead to await the arrival of a supply caravan.

This allowed the Saudis to regroup and fortify themselves anew further down Wadi Hanifah. However, the Samhah fort with its artillery emplacement, on the west bank of the Wadi, soon fell to the Egyptian cavalry under Rishwan Agha and 'Awzun Ali, with further loss of life. The Egyptians then attacked from both sides a tower occupied by 'Umar ibn Saud, the Imam's brother. 'Awzun Ali's cavalry advanced down the two tributaries, Sha'ibs Ghubayrah and Hariqah, to await 'Umar's abandonment of his position. When this happened they attacked Faisal in the rear.

These initial successes at Ghubayrah and Samhah meant that Faisal was now dangerously outflanked. He and his men, with the Imam's brother Sa'd ibn Saud, withdrew further down the wadi through the gardens to the Salmani palm grove. Here they halted, threw back the pursuing enemy, and set up a new defence line across the wadi. The central section was held by the Imam's three brothers, Faisal, Turki and Fahd, and their uncle Abdullah ibn 'Abd al-'Aziz. The west bank of the Wadi was held by another brother, Ibrahim, while above him, in the Ghasibah fort built by Saud the Great with strong iron gates and commanding a good view of the Wadi, was the Imam's son Sa'd with a big gun and a strong force. Farther upstream, the future Imam Turki ibn Abdullah and his son Faisal were posted on the high bank of the

Above: **This village near Shaqra is typical of those through which Ibrahim Pasha passed.**

Durma today preserves some typical examples of Najdi architecture, like this upper reception room. The ceiling cloth, still in place, suggests this house was in use until quite recently.

Below: **The streets of Durma witnessed one of the most savage episodes of Ibrahim Pasha's invasion.**

Left: A street in Durma.

Right: The Imam Abdullah converted Salwa Palace no.1 in Turayf into a storehouse in preparation for the siege. The columns which surrounded the courtyard were embedded in thick walls to make secure store-rooms and magazines.

Ghubayrah tributary. Downstream, the Bulayda tributary, opposite Ghasibah, was held by two more of the Imam's brothers, 'Umar and Hasan. Other brothers, 'Abd al-Rahman and Mishari, held a line between Bulayda and the 'Id prayer ground outside the western wall of Turayf.

More dispositions were made on the east bank of Wadi Hanifah, where Sa'd ibn Saud held the Qulayqil tributary, which runs along the eastern side of Ghasibah, with the Dughaythir brothers. The Imam himself, accompanied by various chiefs and *'ulama'*, stationed himself near Ghasibah, between the Samhan and Zahra gates in a heavily fortified section of the wadi wall.

In the meantime large supply caravans had laboured the hundreds of kilometres across waterless wastes from Basra, Madinah and al-Qasim, with more cavalry and artillery from Cairo. Those wounded at Shaqra who had now recovered rejoined their units. With the Saudi withdrawal down Wadi Hanifah, Ibrahim Pasha moved his camp from 'Ilb to Qari Qusayr, nowadays known in memory of his army as Qurayy al-Rum, a tributary descending from the north. He deployed his troops opposite the defenders' new line of defence. 'Awzun Ali was stationed on the west bank of Wadi Hanifah, confronting those defending the heights of Turayf. Morale rose, and a Saudi assault on the Egyptian left wing commanded by Rishwan Agha was repelled. But perhaps the invaders relaxed too much: Abdullah continued to throw up walls and dig defensive ditches along the new line without harrassment. Ibrahim became impatient with the delay and ordered an attack on the bastions of the Ghasibah gardens. With Vaissière in charge, artillery was positioned and a breach made. But Egyptian morale had evidently faltered. The commander refused to order the assault, blaming the men's reluctance, while the men claimed that their commanders refused to lead them.

Like Achilles before Troy, the enraged Pasha took to his tent in a sulk. A despatch to Muhammad Ali, reporting this insubordination and requesting yet more men, was sent on its precarious two-month journey to Cairo. In response, his father prepared to despatch Khalil Pasha with three thousand cavalry and foot-soldiers. There is little doubt that Ibrahim regarded this as a threat to his own position, and he became ever more anxious at his inability to deliver the *coup de grâce*. As the Imam Abdullah had anticipated, the Egyptian force was too small to besiege Dir'iyyah effectively. The sense of impasse and isolation was being increased as the unusually cold and wet spring gave way to the torrid Najdi summer.

Saudi attacks on the Egyptian camp were intensified, but beaten off with enough losses to persuade some outside suppliers to divert their caravans from Dir'iyyah to the invader. By this time Ibrahim must have woken up fully to the fact that as long as Dir'iyyah was being constantly supplied from the south, without Egyptian opposition, his hopes of a swift end to the campaign were slim. But he could do little about it. May dragged into June as the fighting continued around the main points in the defence such as the Salmani palm grove and the ruins of the Samhah fort, but the stalemate continued. Egyptian losses mounted; sickness and heat-stroke took their toll. Abdullah's men kept up the pressure, forcing the invading soldiery to stay under arms in the heat for five to six hours a day. Under such conditions the misery of the soldiers' lives must have been intense.

Then, on 21st June, slow attrition gave way to calamity. It seems that a whirlwind snatched sparks from a soldier's fire and deposited them in the middle of Ibrahim's ammunition dump. There was a cataclysmic explosion as two hundred barrels of powder went up. Tents, artillery ammunition, wheat and barley stores were all destroyed. The fireworks continued for about ten minutes as 240 cases of cartridges, shells and other ammunition exploded. There were blackened limbs and bodies scattered about, and terrible burns on survivors. Despite efforts to put the fire out, half the army's supplies were lost. The only ammunition left was what the soldiers still had in their pouches, and about nine hundred artillery cartridges and three hundred shells in the gun batteries.

A lesser man than Ibrahim Pasha might have been overcome by despair. To some, however, having nothing to lose is the ultimate stimulus. Although a man of only twenty-six years old, he rose above this misfortune with remarkable fortitude. "All is lost," he is reported to have said, "We have nothing but our courage and our swords with which to attack the enemy." He stiffened his commanders' resolve just in time to repulse an exploratory Saudi assault on the camp. When the Saudis saw that the Egyptians were undaunted, they fell back. The Imam summoned his counsellors, and it was decided to mount a more concerted assault the next day.

Meanwhile Ibrahim urged his men not to use their ammunition unless absolutely necessary, and not to yield an inch on pain of death. Not for the first time the Egyptian soldier must have wondered who was most life-threatening, the enemy or his own leader; yet the effect was salutary. The Saudi assault did indeed come the next day. Fifteen hundred men of Dir'iyyah approached the Egyptian camp, but instead of holding off to test whether the enemy would squander his ammunition, they went straight in for the attack. Ibrahim, watching from rising ground, gave orders to his men to hold fire until the Saudis were upon them, and then to loose off a last-minute fusillade. The tactic worked. The Saudis fell back, leaving many dead and wounded.

This episode was perhaps the turning-point. A second assault might have carried the day, but the effect was to discourage the Imam and make him resume the defensive. Ibrahim had time to summon more supplies and ammunition from the Arabian garrisons, and threw himself into the task of reviving his men, who were falling prey every day to dysentery. Ophthalmia was another serious problem. He himself was afflicted, and had to supervise operations with blinded and streaming eyes. At last, after twenty-five days, supply caravans began to arrive.

At this point, in the heat of late July, Ibrahim changed his tactics. He now seems to have satisfied himself that unless he laid more effective siege to Dir'iyyah success would elude him. Faisal al-Dawish, chief of the Mutayr, gave him intelligence on the villages which were sending supplies regularly to Dir'iyyah. On the strength of this, on the night of 15th August, Ibrahim went with a detachment of two thousand men round to the south of Dir'iyyah and took the village of 'Irqah, in Wadi Hanifah (just by the Diplomatic Quarter today). By garrisoning 'Irqah he hoped to seal off Dir'iyyah from both north and south.

During Ibrahim's two-day absence the Imam Abdullah, who seems to have been kept well informed about the Pasha's movements, attacked the Egyptian camp. The fighting was fierce. In the intense heat the Saudi women were seen braving the gunfire to bring water to their men. Gentili's foot was blown off. But eventually the Saudis were repulsed. Reinforcements and supplies kept arriving at the Egyptian camp and morale was rising. Added to that, Ibrahim received news that Khalil Pasha was on his way. Not wanting to be up-staged, he resolved to tighten the noose on Dir'iyyah by pressing down the wadi from the north.

Bombardment of the fortifications was redoubled. The Imam's brother Faisal, at the head of reconnaissance patrol, was picked off by a sharp-shooter. Ibrahim decided on a night attack, infiltrating eight hundred of his men under 'Awzun Ali behind the defenders by an unguarded lane along a tributary, probably in Bulayda opposite Ghasibah, into the Mushayrifah gardens. The Trojan Horse was within the gates. The defenders were occupied by diversionary Egyptian attacks on the opposite bank, and by the cavalry advancing down the middle of the wadi. The Imam's men were attacked in the rear and retreated in confusion, while the Egyptians took up position before Ghasibah and the Ghasibah fort commanded by Sa'd ibn Abdullah. Saudi casualties were high, including men of note such as Muhammad ibn Mishari, the Imam's brother-in-law, and others of his relatives.

Sa'd's fort with its artillery and 150 men capitulated on the third day, and Sa'd gave himself up. Ibrahim now ordered the bombardment of the two large settlements of Ghasibah and Sahl. Confident of success, he wanted to spare his men's lives and did not order a direct assault. The desperate people of Ghasibah and Sahl followed the example of

Philby's famous photograph of Turayf in 1917 *(below)* from across the wadi is contrasted with the scene from exactly the same spot today *(left)* with the restored Palace of Sa'd dominating and the author seated.

Rass by surrendering on condition that their walls would not be entered until after the capture of Turayf. Meanwhile Ibrahim, in occupying the Mushayrifah palm groves south of Bulayda, had gained access to the bluff of Turayf from the heights to the west. Detachments were posted round Turayf, and Saud ibn Abdullah, the ex-governor of Durma, was captured while trying to escape with some of his men. Accused by Ibrahim of breaking his word, he was put to death.

The Pasha was now able to train his artillery unopposed on Turayf and Turfiyyah. In losing Ghasibah the defenders had lost control of the wadi bed, and so were hopelessly isolated within their walls. Artillery pounded Turayf without opposition, while the embattled Imam tried desperately to rally his people. When Turfiyyah fell, the Imam yielded to the pleas of the exhausted inhabitants. Hoisting the flag of peace on 9th September, he sent an envoy to Ibrahim to request an armistice and conference, to which the Pasha agreed.

THE SURRENDER OF DIR'IYYAH, SEPTEMBER 1818

A few hours later the Imam presented himself at the Pasha's tent, accompanied by two hundred of his followers. Various tales, some of them contradictory, have survived from this dramatic encounter. Captain G.F. Sadleir, on his official mission from the Government of India to the Pasha in 1819, was told that the victorious Ibrahim was extremely haughty, presenting his hand to the Imam who, though some twenty-five years his senior and not yet formally surrendered, kissed it as a sign of submission. Sadleir, who was on the spot a few months later and able to hear first-hand accounts, is probably reliable as a source.

On his way across Arabia Sadleir was to form a low opinion of Ibrahim, whom he accuses of arrogance, barbarous cruelty, bad faith towards his victims, mistreatment of his allies, and general avarice. It is certainly true that Ibrahim could be ruthless. In a political landscape where loyalties were as shifting as the desert sands, success could only be achieved by those with a fine judgment of how to serve their own best interests. But Ibrahim certainly knew how to inspire and repay loyalty, and was capable of magnanimity as well as brutality. For a young man of twenty-six he was a fair judge of when to apply the whip and when to cajole.

French sources paint a more lenient picture of Ibrahim than Sadleir and give fuller details of the meeting. According to one, the vanquished Imam offered to kiss the Pasha's hand, but Ibrahim demurred, bidding him instead to be seated. He is even said to have offered the Imam, though this is hard to believe, munitions to continue the fight. Abdullah, near to tears, is reported to have replied: "No, my lord; God has favoured your arms. It is not your soldiers who have defeated me, it is He who has wished to humble me." Ibrahim then tried to console him with the thought that many other great men had been brought low by ill-fortune. When the Imam asked for peace, Ibrahim agreed but said that he could not leave him at Dir'iyyah, because he was under orders to send him to Cairo; but that he would be responsible for his safety as far as there. Once in Cairo his father would decide whether or not he should be sent on to await the Sultan's pleasure in Istanbul.

Abdullah's response was fatalistic but brave. He is said to have answered: "You are a great man, Ibrahim Pasha, your father is greater than you, and Sultan Mahmoud is greater still than your father; but God is much greater than all of you, and if it is not destined that I should lose my head, nothing will be able to remove it from my shoulders." He then asked for twenty-four hours to consider Ibrahim's terms and consult his advisers.

The request was granted and, after coffee, the Imam departed with his son Sa'd restored to him. The French account, if true, illustrates the common historical truth that enemy leaders often treat each other with more consideration than they do their own men.

It is said that the Pasha spent the night in a state of high anxiety, worrying lest the Imam should use this breathing-space to flee, or even – an unthinkable thing for a devout Muslim – to commit suicide. Guards were posted around Turayf.

However, the Imam had decided that by fleeing he might bring down destruction upon his family and Dir'iyyah itself. He had also formed a favourable opinion of Ibrahim, and took the brave decision to give himself up to be sent into exile and possible death. Once again Ibrahim received him in his tent, where the Imam told him of his decision to go into exile provided that his life was guaranteed. The Pasha replied that he could commit neither Muhammad Ali nor the Sultan, but that he believed both of them too generous to put him to death. The Imam requested pardon for the troops who had remained loyal to him, and for his family, brothers and their families. Ibrahim granted this, but made no commitment to the Imam's other request that Dir'iyyah should not be destroyed.

The next days were spent by the Imam putting his affairs in order, bidding farewell to his weeping family and, it seems, occasionally dining with Ibrahim, who continued to treat him with distinction. The fallen Imam left with his personal secretary and his most faithful slaves, and was escorted by four hundred of Ibrahim's men on the fateful two-month progress across Arabia before the eyes of his former subjects, and across the Red Sea. He arrived in Cairo on 17th November. Great celebrations had been planned, part of

This impressive old fort in the Bulayda area commands one of the tributaries joining Wadi Hanifah, and was probably the scene of savage fighting. Today, it is used as a farmyard.

which was to be a fortress built by the Nile representing Dir'iyyah. Here the siege was to be re-enacted with the Saudi captives on public display inside.

Sources do not confirm whether these indignities actually took place. By all accounts Muhammad Ali received the Imam kindly. However he sent him off after only two days to Istanbul, with a recommendation to Sultan Mahmoud for a pardon. Whether the Imam was prepared for the humiliation to follow is not known. He was paraded through the streets of the Ottoman capital for three days amid celebrations, like a vanquished leader in a Roman triumph. Several Turkish *'ulama'* tried to convince him of the error of his beliefs but, brave man that he was, he would not be shaken from the doctrines of *tawhid*. Then, in late November 1818, he was beheaded in public, at the gate of the gardens of the Serai. After the execution his head was crushed in a mortar and his body suspended on a post. The death sentence, impaled on a dagger plunged into his body, was on public view for all to see.

To the last the Imam Abdullah ibn Saud was as much a martyr to the reform movement as a defeated leader of his people. Though the fall of Dir'iyyah and the execution of its Imam meant the end of the First Saudi State, the spirit of the reform movement was only briefly crushed in Najd. Dir'iyyah's mantle passed to Riyadh in 1824 under a revived Saudi dynasty, and its influence is still essential to the character of the Kingdom to this day.

Chapter Eight

Final Vengeance

The city is razed

The capitulation of Dir'iyyah in September 1818 marked the end of the First Saudi State. Ibrahim Pasha was not only master of Najd; he takes his place in history as its first-ever, and its only, conqueror from outside Arabia. The Pasha's victory was decidedly Pyrrhic – a portent for any attempt to occupy Najd – for Ibn Bishr tells us that his campaign had cost the lives of twelve thousand men, the great majority in the fighting for Dir'iyyah, while the defenders lost only twelve hundred.

After the surrender, Ibrahim struck camp and his men moved into the abandoned houses of Turayf. But Ibrahim's position was hardly secure. He was a thousand miles from Cairo, and isolated at the end of a long and precarious supply line. Despite the heavy rains of 1818 and 1819, Najd was never anything but a barren land, and its agriculture had been severely disrupted by the war and the cutting down of palms outside towns which had resisted. With the removal of Dir'iyyah's central authority, tribe and town dissolved into anarchy. Families and tribes lost their trust in each other, old scores were settled, and banditry broke out again. People could no longer sleep safe in their houses. Famine stalked the land, afflicting invader and occupied alike. It is said that at one time Ibrahim's men were reduced to eating grass. On another occasion a thousand angry soldiers gathered in the great square of Dir'iyyah, but Ibrahim confronted the mob in person and calmed them by undertaking to send them back as soon as a relief column arrived from Madinah. He was not too proud to take part himself in foraging expeditions.

Meanwhile, he had to organise the occupation while awaiting orders from Muhammad Ali. Ibrahim always presented himself as his father's dutiful son and willing servant, and his father as carrying out the orders of the Sultan in Istanbul. It is quite possible that, despite his growing imperial ambitions, Muhammad Ali did not intend at this point a permanent occupation of Najd. Ibrahim did send a small detachment of troops to take control of al-Hasa and Qatif, but this was to obtain supplies. The campaign and its aftermath would have shown that the practical and human costs of occupation were too high. What is certain is that Muhammad Ali was bent on the complete destruction of Najd and the reform movement as a political force, following the Roman principle of creating a desert and calling it peace. This done, he would try to exert indirect control of Najd through local puppet rulers who recognised his authority. This would achieve his chief aim: the long-term security of the Holy Cities.

While Ibrahim awaited his father's instructions, he dealt harshly with representatives of the old order. Ex-governors, divines and other notables had their beards shaved off and their teeth pulled out. Some were tortured and, in extreme cases, tied to the mouth of a cannon which was then fired. Ruling families in al-Qasim and al-Kharj were deprived of their leading members. Many Najdis fled to the Gulf, and others emigrated as far afield as North Africa.

In May 1819 orders arrived from Muhammad Ali to evacuate Najd, restrict the occupation to the Hijaz, and deport all the remaining prominent members of the House of Saud and the Al al-Shaykh, who had not escaped the net, to Cairo. About four hundred men, women and children were collected to make the forlorn and arduous journey into Egyptian exile, where they were pensioned off by Muhammad Ali.

Included in the orders was the instruction to destroy Dir'iyyah. We are lucky to have a first-hand witness of the results of the razing of the capital, for into this scene of despair and desolation stepped, in 1819, the unlikely figure of an officer of the British army in India. Captain George Forster Sadleir was sent from Bombay to establish contact with Ibrahim Pasha in Arabia, and to sound him out about the possibility of cooperating with the British in the suppression of the anarchy in the southern Gulf that was stifling local commerce, and still bedevilling imperial communications between India and London. This hope was based on the assumption that the Egyptians intended to occupy central and eastern Arabia.

As Sadleir soon realised, the hope of Egyptian occupation was a false one. He arrived at Qatif and al-Hasa Oasis just as the evacuation of the small Egyptian detachment was making it plain that Ibrahim contemplated no such thing. But he resolved nonetheless to fulfil his mission, and accompanied one of the evacuating convoys from al-Hasa. He arrived at Manfuhah, just by Riyadh, on 3rd August 1819.

Sadleir tells us that Ibrahim did not make the order to destroy Dir'iyyah public until he had extorted as much money as he could from the remaining inhabitants as ransom for their persons and property. His men meanwhile pillaged as much as they could. After this act of bad faith, he gave orders for the demolition of the town. His men set fire to the buildings, starting with the palace of Imam Abdullah and the mosques, without a care for the occupants of neighbouring buildings. Some of the time the people themselves were forced into the work of destruction. The soldiers cut down all of Dir'iyyah's palms, making their own speedy evacuation essential. Ibn Bishr remarks despairingly that they left it looking as if no one had lived there since ancient times. When Sadleir came on the scene in August 1819, he could not find a single person among the ruins, and all the date palms, vines, apricot, fig, lemon and pomegranate trees had been laid low. Only a few tamarisk trees remained. This was in contrast to Riyadh and Manfuhah where he had observed, during his three-day halt there, that while the walls had been razed the palm groves were still intact, and sheltered many of Dir'iyyah's now homeless former inhabitants.

Sadleir was in a position to observe the results of Ibrahim's evacuation of Najd at first-hand. The tracks of the Pasha's artillery were still visible down the Haysiyyah pass beyond 'Uyaynah. Tharmida's walls had been razed, and Marat was in ruins. The town of Shaqra was in good repair, and its date groves flourishing, although its walls had been demolished. 'Unayzah was in ruins, and many of its palms cut down. When he reached Rass, he was dismayed to find that Ibrahim had left for Madinah just two days before. He decided to continue his dogged pursuit of the Pasha, finally catching up with him at Madinah. Negotiations with Ibrahim in Jeddah turned out unsuccessfully, but in the process Sadleir had unintentionally become the first European to cross Arabia from coast to coast.

Ibrahim had evacuated in stages, first making a new headquarters at Durma, leaving a detachment at Dir'iyyah, and conducting forays against the 'Ujman and 'Anazah bedouin, who would have interfered with his retreating columns. A second group of Al Saud was sent on to Cairo, to be pensioned by Muhammad Ali. Local governors were made responsible for the destruction of town walls and forts which had hitherto been spared. Ibrahim then moved on to Shaqra, called up the Dir'iyyah detachment, and moved on to al-Qasim, having made a final round of inspection to check that fortifications had been razed according to his orders. He reached Madinah in September, and by December was back home in Cairo, where he was received with seven days of lavish celebrations.

DIR'IYYAH RE-OCCUPIED

The story of Dir'iyyah does not quite end with its destruction by Ibrahim Pasha. Ibrahim seems to have made no arrangements to instal puppet rulers in southern Najd, even going back on his promise to make Faisal al-Dawish of the Mutayr governor of Dir'iyyah. After the withdrawal from Najd, Muhammad Ali's "Governor of Arabia", Ahmad Pasha, concentrated on consolidating Egyptian rule of the Hijaz and Holy Cities. Ibrahim had left Najd in a state of anarchy and ruin. Despite the rains of 1818 and 1819, food was short and prices cripplingly high. Lawlessness and disunity prevailed: Najd at that time seemed to present no threat outside its borders.

However, despite Muhammad Ali's hopes that the House of Saud and the reform movement had been quashed once and for all, a succession of individuals came forward in the years 1819-24 to try to restore order and fill the political vacuum. This was to culminate in the rise to power of Turki ibn Abdullah ibn Muhammad ibn Saud, a cousin of Saud the Great, and one of Dir'iyyah's most doughty defenders during the siege.

The first of these attempts to resurrect the reformist state involved an attempt to re-build Dir'iyyah. As early as September 1819 Muhammad ibn Mishari ibn Mu'ammar, of the old ruling house of 'Uyaynah, proceeded to Dir'iyyah to proclaim himself Imam and ruler of Najd. As a relative of Al Saud on his mother's side, and a participant in the defence of Dir'iyyah against Ibrahim Pasha, he drew support. Already by the end of 1819 he had organised re-building some of the capital.

By this time the Banu Khalid had re-established their rule of al-Hasa, and their chief Majid ibn 'Urai'ir had his eyes on filling the Najdi vacuum himself. Acting on an invitation from Riyadh, al-Kharj and Huraymila, which in their time had all been at enmity with the House of Saud, he reached the environs of Riyadh with a bedouin force. Ibn Mu'ammar had moved in the meantime to Manfuhah to confront him. After some half-hearted fighting peace was arranged. Ibn Mu'ammar warned Majid that his rule in Najd was in the name of the Ottoman Sultan, and it may indeed be true that in pursuing power in Najd he had already taken the precaution of offering nominal submission to the Egyptians.

Ibn Mu'ammar's small success before Riyadh raised his prestige. Turki ibn Abdullah, the future Imam, had escaped the Egyptian net at the fall of Dir'iyyah, and now emerged from hiding to help restore unity.

Then, in early 1820, another claimant to the rule surfaced. Mishari ibn Saud, a brother of the executed Imam Abdullah, had managed to give his guards the slip on the way to Egypt. Now suddenly he re-appeared in Sudayr, gathering followers, and descended on the devastated capital. As a true member of the ruling house Mishari had a more widespread appeal than Ibn Mu'ammar, whose support suddenly melted away and went over to the new arrival. Turki followed suit. Ibn Mu'ammar accepted the inevitable and pledged his loyalty to the new Imam, but his submission was reluctant. Under Mishari the re-building of Dir'iyyah continued, and he occupied the palace which still bears his name. He appointed Turki governor of Riyadh, whose walls had been re-built and which was in a good state of repair.

The news reached Cairo. Muhammad Ali had decided that the Saudi resurgence threatened his plan of indirect rule, and gave orders that Najd should be occupied once more. Ibn Mu'ammar retired to Sadus and Huraymila to intrigue against Mishari. Gathering a force which included the pro-Egyptian Faisal al-Dawish and his Mutayr tribesmen, he led a surprise march on Dir'iyyah which he entered unopposed. He went to Mishari's palace and took the Imam prisoner, and then seized Riyadh, whose governor Turki had fled. At this point, an Egyptian force from the Hijaz entered al-Qasim in support of Ibn Mu'ammar, and its commander confirmed him as ruler, so making it plain for all to see that Ibn Mu'ammar was indeed a quisling of Muhammad Ali.

Turki was equal to the situation. Making Durma his base of operations, he evaded capture by a detachment under Ibn Mu'ammar's son, whom he forced to flee. In December 1820 Turki marched on Dir'iyyah and

Caption overleaf

surprised Ibn Mu'ammar, taking him prisoner. Next he marched on Riyadh and captured Ibn Mu'ammar's son. He offered to release them if their supporters in Sadus freed the Imam Mishari. In the event, they were unable to comply because the Egyptians had just reached Sadus, and the Imam was turned over to them by Ibn Mu'ammar's supporters. Mishari died in 'Unayzah while being sent once again to captivity in Egypt.

Turki's response to this was to make good his threat to kill Ibn Mu'ammar and his son. The Egyptian troops in Sadus now pressed forward, and Turki, making Riyadh his base, prepared to defend it. At first he succeeded, and the Egyptians retired to Tharmida, where they set up their new base for the occupation of Najd.

But in late 1820 things took a turn for the worse when a new Egyptian commander, the infamous Husayn Bey, arrived in Tharmida. He attacked Riyadh, forcing Turki to flee. This time Turki lay low in al-Kharj, not to reappear before Riyadh until 1824.

What followed was a second reign of terror, more extreme even than Ibrahim Pasha's. Husayn Bey, who deserves a prominent place in the demonology of foreign occupiers, set about the destruction of Najdi political, economic and intellectual life anew. In March 1821 he ordered all the inhabitants of Dir'iyyah to leave. Those who resisted were taken to Tharmida where a kind of concentration camp had been prepared for them, ostensibly till they could be re-settled elsewhere in Najd. No less than 230 of the men were then butchered on Husayn Bey's orders.

Their remaining property was stolen, and the survivors were kept as hostages. Once again, the Egyptians demolished the re-built Dir'iyyah, which had obviously retained its potency as a symbol of the reform movement. They plundered what was left of Najd, carrying out wholesale extortions, mutilations, killings, book burnings and the cutting down of palm trees. Proponents of reform were particularly targeted and the Al al-Shaykh suffered extreme persecution.

This episode marks the end of Dir'iyyah's story as a capital. Turayf was abandoned for good: Palgrave in 1862 and Pelly in 1865 both found it utterly deserted. Good farmland does not go uncultivated in Najd, however, and the oasis of Dir'iyyah has been settled and farmed continuously ever since. In 1917 Philby found Turayf completely deserted still, but estimated the number of inhabitants of the oasis as a whole, living in their small farming villages and amongst the gardens, at seven thousand. In the middle decades of the 20th century an effort was made to re-settle Turayf, and the mass of courtyard houses which fills the eastern end of the site belong to this time. When Violet Dickson, wife of the late Harold Dickson with whom she had visited Dir'iyyah in 1937, re-visited the site in 1962, the building of these houses was well under way. They are in much better condition than the 18th and early 19th century remains among which they were built. The mud from the ruins was used to make new mud bricks and mortar and, in some cases, original doors from the older houses were installed in the new ones. These houses were abandoned by their last inhabitants in about 1982.

Above right: **The eastern portion of Turayf, shown here, was re-occupied in the mid-20th century, and houses were built among the old palaces, re-using the mud from the ruins. Wadi Hanifah's palm groves snake off into the distance; Sha'ib Safar joins it from the right.**

Left: **Both the Dicksons and the Rendels visited Dir'iyyah in 1937. This picture by George Rendel shows a well-preserved palace which is now hard to identify.**

Previous page: **This, the earliest known photograph of Turayf, was taken by the British traveller Gerard Leachman in 1912.**

THE IMAM TURKI REVIVES DIR'IYYAH'S TRADITION

When Husayn Bey's tour of duty came to an end in 1821, he left three garrisons in Najd: one at 'Unayzah, one at Tharmida, and the third at the town which was now emerging as the obvious choice as the centre for control of southern Najd, Riyadh. The harshness of the new occupation lost the Egyptians any local support they once had. When Turki emerged from hiding in 1823, events flowed in his favour, and by 1824 he was able to force out the Egyptian garrison in Riyadh, already beleaguered by an Egyptian blunder in al-Qasim. Once again Muhammad Ali's troops evacuated southern Najd and al-Qasim and withdrew to the Hijaz.

Dir'iyyah's second abandonment in 1821 had clearly rendered it an unattractive prospect for re-building. It may also have been anxiety not to provoke Muhammad Ali which helped to determine the new Imam's choice of Riyadh as the new seat of government: it had probably not gone unheeded that re-buildings of Dir'iyyah were synonymous in the Egyptian mind with the resurgence of the House of Saud. In any case, Riyadh was a well-maintained garrison town. With Najd once more free of the invader, Turki set about consolidating his rule.

Refugees returned, and a new era dawned in Najd, dimmed only by a third Egyptian invasion and occupation in 1837-40. The Second Saudi State with its capital at Riyadh only forms part of our story insofar as the spiritual legacy of Dir'iyyah determined the nature of the revived central authority.

The Imam Turki and his son Faisal, who was to succeed him in 1834, were in the tradition of the great Saudi rulers. The rule of law was re-established, and the desert once more became safe. The character of their rule emerges most strongly from an address delivered by the Imam Turki to a great gathering of his governors and chiefs at Hofuf in 1832. Ibn Bishr records it as follows:

> He said, "Verily, whenever my order reaches you for a raid, you lay increased burdens on the people for your own benefit. Take care not to do that, for nothing prevents me from putting on the people ... an increased claim for camels in the raids except compassion for them, and I lay on them a smaller claim than he who preceded me used to lay on them. ... Verily, whenever my order reaches you, you are happy about it because you find something in it for yourselves. You are like those who watch a palm tree and rejoice when a strong wind blows because more dates fall. Now know that I shall not allow you to take anything from the people. He among you who commits injustice toward his flock, his punishment will not be dismissal but exile from his country." Then he said to the people, "If any amir oppresses you, inform me of it." Then the governor of Buraydah, 'Abd al-'Aziz ibn Muhammad ibn Abdullah ibn Hasan, stood up and said, "O Imam of the Muslims, be specific, and not general in your speech. If you have been angry at any one of us, tell him of his deeds." Then Turki said, "The speech refers only to you and those like you who believe you possess these districts by your swords, while actually they were taken and subdued for you by the sword of Islam and because you agreed on an Imam."

These ringing words form a fitting epilogue to the story of Dir'iyyah. A town may be destroyed, trees cut down, crops and books may be burnt, but an idea capturing hearts and minds is more durable than any thing. The reform movement was of course essentially intolerant of difference, and its adherents were often bent more on material than spiritual advancement. The consequences of these failings when it came into collision with the outside world could be brutal. Despite that, in its tribal heartland and when led by a just Imam, it was an essentially civilising force. It sought to overcome the petty divisions between men, and to bring internal peace, by inspiring a commitment to a larger ideal: the community of man under God.

الدرعيّة

CHAPTER NINE

Mud and Stone

Building techniques and preservation

DIR'IYYAH'S UNIQUENESS

In both style and construction techniques Turayf, the chief town and citadel of Dir'iyyah, stands apart from other Najdi towns. No other contemporary settlement in central Arabia, with the possible exception of 'Unayzah, possessed buildings of such grandeur, and the palaces of the ruling family during Dir'iyyah's apogee in the 18th and early 19th centuries presented a uniquely imposing architecture. This style of building does not appear to have survived Dir'iyyah's destruction. The prosperity of the First Saudi State seems to have prompted the development of a distinctive type of architecture, in which the use of stone and mud was refined to a high degree, and which seems to have died with it.

The palaces of members of the ruling house, which are today named after their final occupants, were solidly built structures, squarish in plan, and usually laid out round a central courtyard. They varied from single-storey structures, like the restored Palace of Nasr, to two-storey courtyard palaces like the Palace of Sa'd, and three- and four-storey blocks like the Salwa Palaces, which were taller than they were wide.

A special feature of the palaces was the so-called toilet tower or long-drop privy. Each palace had two, at opposite corners, and sometimes each privy was divided into two. Because they were robustly built four-square "chimneys", these have tended to survive better than the adjacent walls of which they formed a part, and so stand out like spires today. Originally the palace walls rose to the same height as the toilet towers, which were not therefore conspicuous. It is said that only one toilet tower was used at a time, for half the year. It was then sealed, cleared out through a door at the bottom, and the contents dried and used as fertiliser, as in the Yemen.

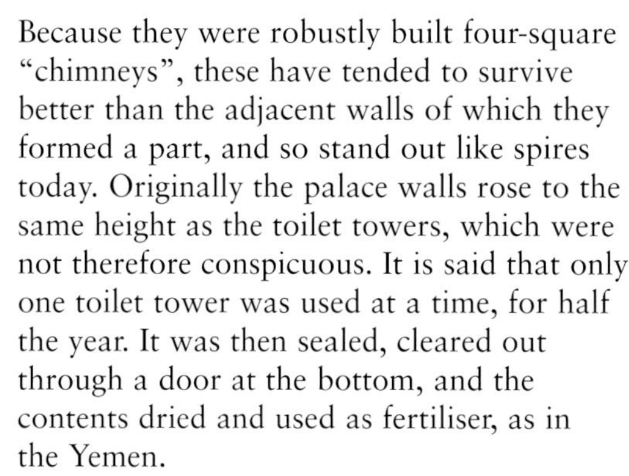

The thick external walls of the palaces, like those of all Najdi buildings, presented an essentially featureless face to the outside world, except where they were perforated on upper levels by patterns of ventilation holes in the form of triangles and lancets. Many of the walls surviving today help to preserve the forbidding impression which Dir'iyyah's great buildings must once have made on its people and visitors to the court of Al Saud.

CONSTRUCTION TECHNIQUES

Like all Najdi towns, the building material of Turayf is to a large extent of sun-dried mud brick. However, it is unlike other Najdi towns in the amount of stone used in its construction. Stone was commonly used in Najdi buildings to provide a foundation, sometimes rising to a few feet above ground level. The stone courses were then covered with mud plaster like the mud-brick superstructure, so that they were not visible. In common with the rest of Najd, stone was also used in Dir'iyyah in the construction of columns. Limestone blocks were fashioned into drums which would then be laid one on another. The finished column would then be covered with mud plaster. In a building of two storeys the column would be run continuously to the full height of the upper storey beams. Another common use of stone was in the construction of keel arches to make the arcades in mosques: here two slabs of stone would be leant together from the tops of adjacent columns, to form the apex of the arch where they met.

But at Dir'iyyah, stone was often also used to construct entire walls. In the western half of the site, where the common people of Turayf are thought to have lived, this can be seen clearly today. Rough cut, flat blocks of the plentiful local limestone are laid on edge in mud mortar, at an angle of 45°, to form courses of masonry, sometimes laid in a herringbone pattern. The walls were then plastered over, so that their stone construction would not have been visible when the buildings were in use. In other cases, courses of stone

Left: **The toilet tower of the Palace of Saud the Great rises behind a section of the Salwa Palaces' wall, built of mud layers.**

Right: **Long-drop privies, like this one in the Palace of 'Umar, had narrow entrances.**

Far right: **This toilet tower served the Palace of 'Umar.**

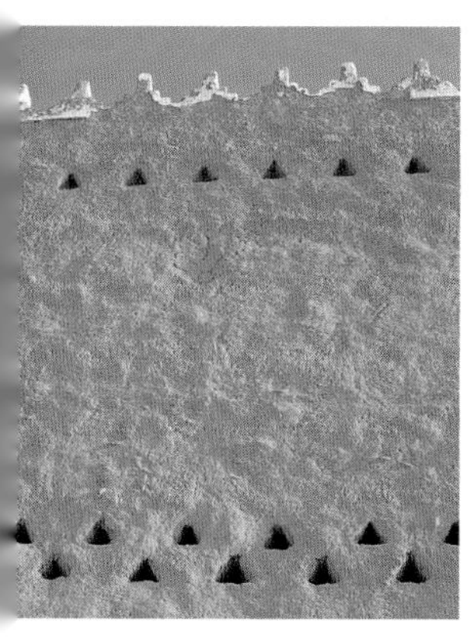

Above left: Pierced triangles and lancets can be found next to the Palace of Abdullah.

Above: This part of the outer wall of the Palace of Sa'd has been restored.

Right: This view shows the western part of Turayf, where rough-cut stone was used to build walls to their full height.

alternate with courses of mud brick.

In addition to this, dressed stone blocks were used extensively at Dir'iyyah in the construction of the lower courses of the great palaces, such as the Salwa Palaces and the Palace of Thunayyan. Such fine masonry work is not found elsewhere in Najd.

But Dir'iyyah's chief architectural glory lies in the way mud brick was used to build the palaces of the ruling house. Once the ground plan of the building had been laid out and the foundations and lower courses constructed in stone blocks, the remaining courses were laid in mud brick. The survival of many of these structures to a considerable height testifies to the durable quality of the mud used to make the bricks, and this in turn testifies to the exacting standards and knowledge of the master builders. The name of at least one of these master builders has survived: the Chief Mason Ibn Hazm, whose house has been identified at the eastern end of Turayf.

Mud construction in Arabia traces its ancestry to pre-Islamic times. It was not only its ready availability that made mud the natural building material in the region. Massive mud walls also provide effective insulation – far more so than concrete. This property of thermal inertia ensures that rooms remain cooler for longer as the day warms up, and remain warm as the night air cools.

The durability of mud walls can vary greatly. The quality of the raw materials available, the

Left: Keel arches and columns, both of stone plastered over, in the Mosque of Subalat Mudi.

The use of stone: herringbone pattern in western Turayf *(right)*.

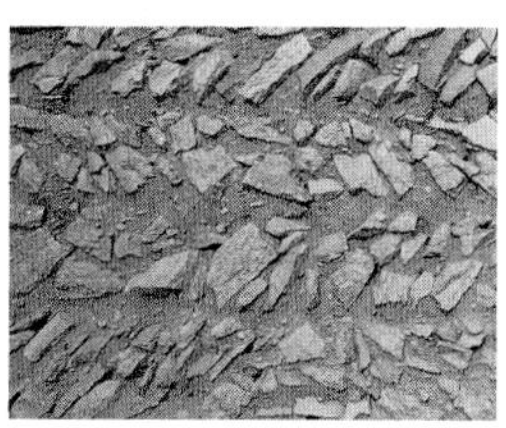

Left: Dressed limestone blocks form the revetment on which the Palace of Thunayyan was constructed.

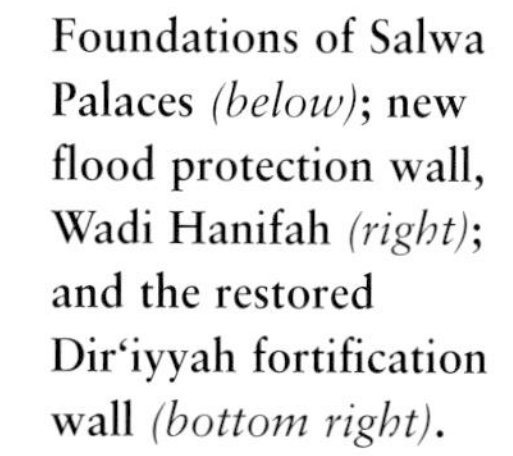

Foundations of Salwa Palaces *(below)*; new flood protection wall, Wadi Hanifah *(right)*; and the restored Dir'iyyah fortification wall *(bottom right)*.

recipe used by the builder, and the care that went into the preparation of the mix, are all factors. The mud mix used in the construction of more recent traditional Najdi buildings, such as the houses built when Turayf was briefly re-occupied in the mid-20th century, seems to be of an inferior quality compared to that used in the preparation of the bricks and mud plaster of the early palaces.

The essential ingredient of mud bricks (*libn*) is clay (*tin*), found in natural deposits in Najd, usually in the presence of ground water. Clay has the necessary adhesiveness to bind into a solid mass, but its stickiness renders it difficult to work with on its own, and a thick mass of clay will crack and break up unless tempered with other materials. To make bricks, therefore, clay was mixed with fine soil (*turab*) taken from silt deposits in wadi banks, and chopped wheat or barley straw (*tibn*, *sha'ir*) would be added. The great excavated pit in the bed of the small wadi which cuts into Turayf below the Palace of Thunayyan shows where much of these materials must have been obtained.

These raw materials were mixed and water was added. After thorough mixing, sometimes by trampling, it could then be used immediately if bricks were to be made. This was done by pouring the mix into a brick-shaped wooden frame on the ground, removing the frame, amd pouring the next one. The bricks were then left in the sun in rows to dry. Alternatively, if the mix was to be used directly for constructing a wall in continuous layers, the mix might be left for several hours to "ferment". It was considered that, the longer the mix was left to ferment in this way, the better the quality of the building material, and it was left for up to twenty-four hours if the mix was to be used for a fine mud plaster finish on the completed wall.

Left: New mud bricks are laid out to dry above Mulaybid.

Far left: The mud mix for restoration work is prepared

Below: Clay was dug to build Turayf from this great excavated pit below the house of the chief mason.

Above: Old mud bricks were squarish and of a hard, creamy texture, with the minimum of silt added to the clay.

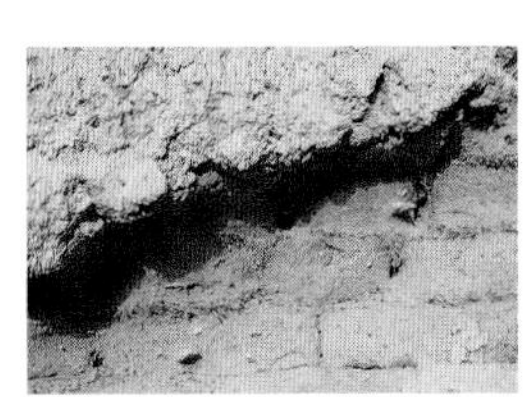

Above: Old mud bricks are carefully laid in straw-rich mortar, Salwa Palace 6.

Left: the wall of Salwa Palace no.1, reducing in thickness with each storey.

The mud bricks used to construct the late 18th and early 19th palaces at Dir'iyyah are of a particularly fine quality. Compared with bricks commonly used in the more recent past, they are large, flat and somewhat square in shape.The mud is rather creamy, with very little gravel, suggesting that only a minimum of fine wadi silt was used to temper the clay. There is hardly any straw in the mix. These observations suggest that the builders wanted to maximise the proportion of clay, for the sake of hardness and durability, and added just enough silt and straw to ensure that the bricks remained crack-free.

The bricks were then used to build up the walls on top of foundations and lower courses of limestone blocks. At the base the walls would be very thick – a metre or more – especially if the building was to be a tall one. For example, the *majlis* of Saud the Great, one of the Salwa Palaces, has a thickness of three mud bricks on the ground floor, two

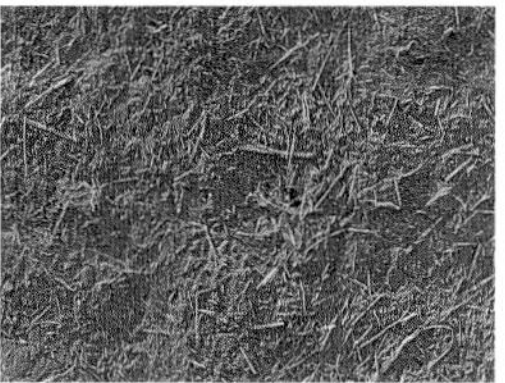

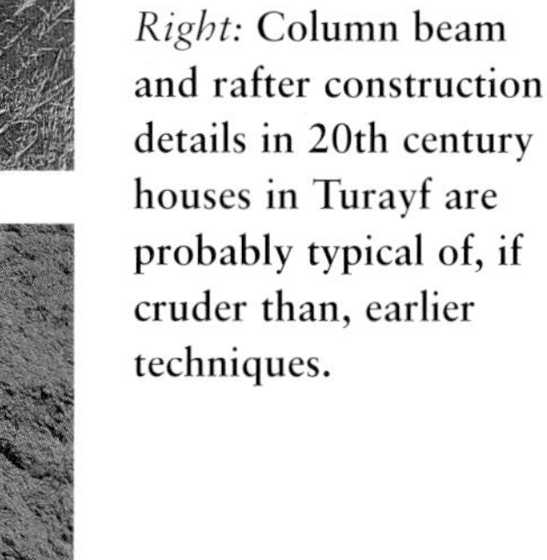
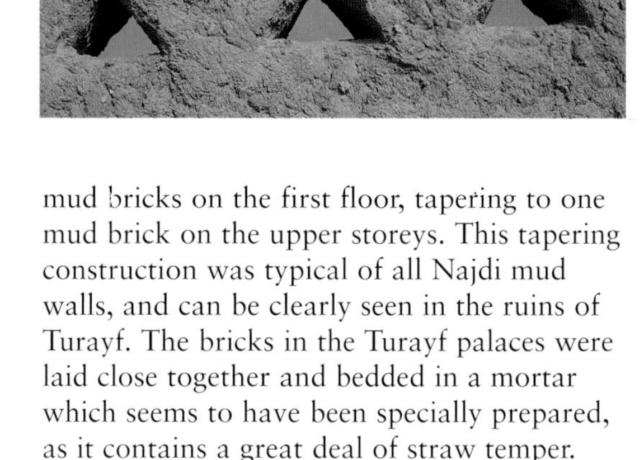

Left: Mud wall textures, Turayf.

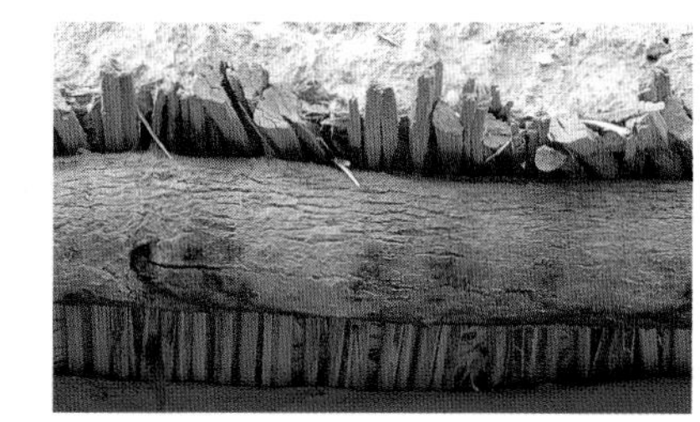
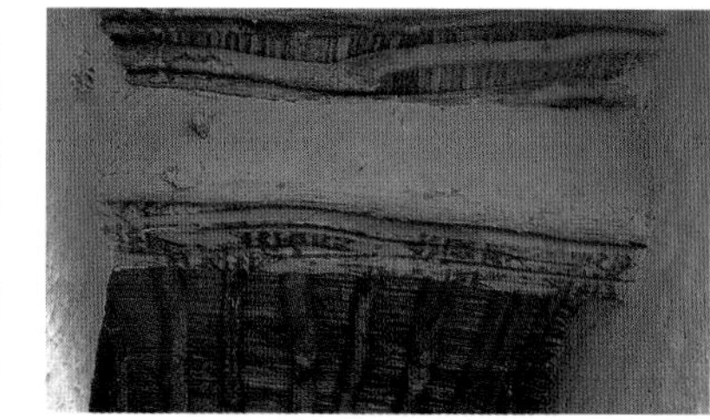

Right: Column beam and rafter construction details in 20th century houses in Turayf are probably typical of, if cruder than, earlier techniques.

mud bricks on the first floor, tapering to one mud brick on the upper storeys. This tapering construction was typical of all Najdi mud walls, and can be clearly seen in the ruins of Turayf. The bricks in the Turayf palaces were laid close together and bedded in a mortar which seems to have been specially prepared, as it contains a great deal of straw temper. Once the building was nearing completion, and the decorative triangular ventilation apertures and lancets pierced through the wall, the building would be plastered.

Another method used to build walls at Dir'iyyah recalls the standard construction method of buildings in the south-west of Saudi Arabia in Bishah, Najran and Dhahran al-Junub, and in Sa'dah in northern Yemen. It is therefore interesting to speculate whether influence from this region affected the evolution of Dir'iyyah's distinctive architecture, particularly in view of the two Najrani expeditions against Dir'iyyah in the 18th century, and the close links with south-west Najd, Asir and Yemen during the heyday of the reform movement. This method, in which the mud mix was used directly to make the wall in continuous, solid layers, each at twenty-four hour intervals, was described by Sadleir at Dir'iyyah in 1819, just after its initial destruction by Ibrahim Pasha. Clearly re-building was already in progress:

> The foundation of the walls was apparently built with large flat stones which are found in abundance in the hills to the north; these were strongly cemented with yellow earth, and of which latter material the upper part of the wall was composed; this earth is very adhesive, and found in abundance all over this part of Arabia; the greater part of the houses are usually built of it. The process of building is very simple. A pit is dug where this earth is expected to be found, and water poured in to mix it into mortar, layers of which are formed of the breadth of the wall by means of a few planks made into the form of a long box; when one layer is completed and dry, another is added, and thus a house is constructed of three or even four stories, the walls of which are one solid mass of this earth, which requires only the labour of the father and his children. Limestone is found near Deriah, but the scarcity of fuel precludes its being brought into use for building, although a sufficiency is procured for white-washing and sometimes for plastering.

Flat stone slabs were laid on tamarisk rafters in Salwa Palace no.1 *(left)* and the Palace of Thunayyan *(right)*.

Timber was used structurally, as in the rest of Najd, to make ceilings and lintels. The wood was almost always tamarisk (*ithl*), though palm trunks might occasionally be used. Tamarisk is light, strong and tensile. It does not split easily, and branches and trunks grow to a sufficient length for use as rafters. Rafters would be laid close together to span a room, or in larger rooms to span across to a central column-supported beam. Palm leaves were then laid over the rafters, and a thick layer of rubble and mud laid on top of that to form the floor above or the roof. Very occasionally, instead of palm leaves and

rubble, flat stone slabs might be laid across the rafters. This can be seen in small rooms in the Salwa Palaces and the Palace of Thunayyan.

Tamarisk or palm planks were used to make doors which, at Dir'iyyah as elsewhere in Najd, were the one building feature which was colourfully decorated, though lintels and cross-beams were also often decorated with patterns of scorched dots and some colour. Many of the original doors were re-used in the mid-20th century re-occupation of Turayf.

Top right: **Al-'Udhaibat Farm is situated at the mouth of Wadi Safar, where it joins Wadi Hanifah. This area was the scene of skirmishes during the siege of Dir'iyyah. The farm later belonged to King Faisal and is now being restored by HRH Prince Sultan ibn Salman ibn 'Abd al-'Aziz.**

These Najdi decorated doors, probably 20th century, at Turayf, are typical*(left and above).*

RESTORATION

In 1974 the Department of Antiquities and Museums became interested in preserving the remains of Dir'iyyah, and UNESCO sponsored a study of the site which was carried out by the Egyptian Antiquities Organisation – a nice historical irony considering the events of 1818-21. By 1978, a second study had been carried out. The aim of both studies was to recommend structures for preservation and restoration, and propose methods for doing so.

The restoration of sun-dried mud buildings involves difficult decisions. Such buildings naturally suffer from heavy rain, and their use entails a commitment to constantly maintain them. Despite research, no modern additive to the mud mix has been found to give a wholly satisfactory result in terms of increased durability. The decision to use only original materials means that a continuing programme of repair of restored buildings has to be undertaken.

A further problem with the restoration of a mud building is that it is almost impossible to tell which part is original, and which re-built or renovated. Mud walls tend to collapse completely into shapeless heaps which tell little about their original appearance except for their alignment. They have to be re-built as new, therefore, and inevitably "restored" structures take on the appearance of brand new buildings. In the process, the atmosphere of age is lost, however much care is taken, as it must be, to use original materials.

The Department of Antiquities has faced this challenge by selecting only certain buildings for restoration – the approach recommended in the UNESCO reports. Inside Turayf, since the 1970s, it has concentrated on restoring first the Palace of Nasr, and then, in the late 1980s, the Palace of Sa'd.

The major effort has been expended on restoring the fortification walls and towers of Turayf, and the great work of re-building the defensive wall lining the heights on either side of Wadi Hanifah from near 'Ilb in the north to Mulaybid in the south is nearing completion. As this goes on, there is also an ongoing programme to repair sections of the walls and buildings which collapse after exceptionally heavy rain storms.

With time, the decision may be taken to re-build other structures inside Turayf, such as the Salwa Palaces, the Bait al-Mal, the Turayf Mosque and the Baths. However, at present it is seen as a priority to consolidate many of the remains as they are, to prevent further deterioration. The Department faces its task with the determination to preserve this historic site for future generations of Saudi Arabians. No visitor, whether Saudi or foreign, can fail to be impressed by the work that has been carried out. In this new phase of its existence, as the great symbol of Saudi Arabian nationhood, Dir'iyyah's survival is assured.

Much of the Department of Antiquities' effort has been spent restoring the great wall of Dir'iyyah: re-building the wall above Mulaybid *(above and left)*, a restored tower west of Turayf *(above right)* and a tower in the Bulayda area *(below)*.

The former Chevron compound at Dir'iyyah, across Wadi Hanifah from Turayf, is famous for its traditionally built Najdi courtyard house, used for recreation and pool changing-rooms.

الدرعيّة

CHAPTER TEN

Dir'iyyah's Turayf Today

A visit to the ruins of Turayf today requires an effort of the imagination. The site still dominates its bluff overlooking Wadi Hanifah but, once inside, it can be difficult for the visitor to recapture its former grandeur. This section focuses on Turayf's most important old buildings, particularly the palaces of the House of Saud.

Right: Turayf from the east, with the Salwa Palaces in the foreground. The road runs along the bed of Wadi Hanifah.

Left and bottom left: Detailed views from the south-west, with the Salwa Palaces in the background. The top picture shows the Palace of Mishari in the foreground.

Below and below right: Detailed views from the north-east, showing 20th century houses among the older buildings. The foreground *(below right)* shows the Salwa Palaces with the Bayt al-Mal (Treasury) to their left, with its curved wall.

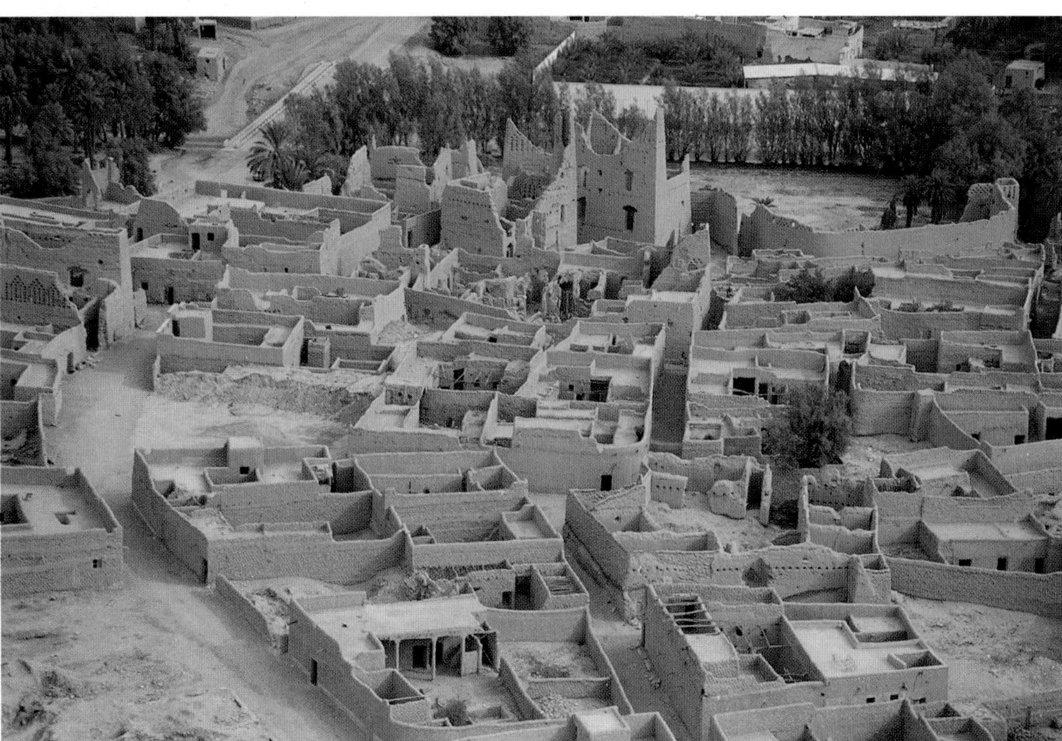

Sketch Plan of Turayf

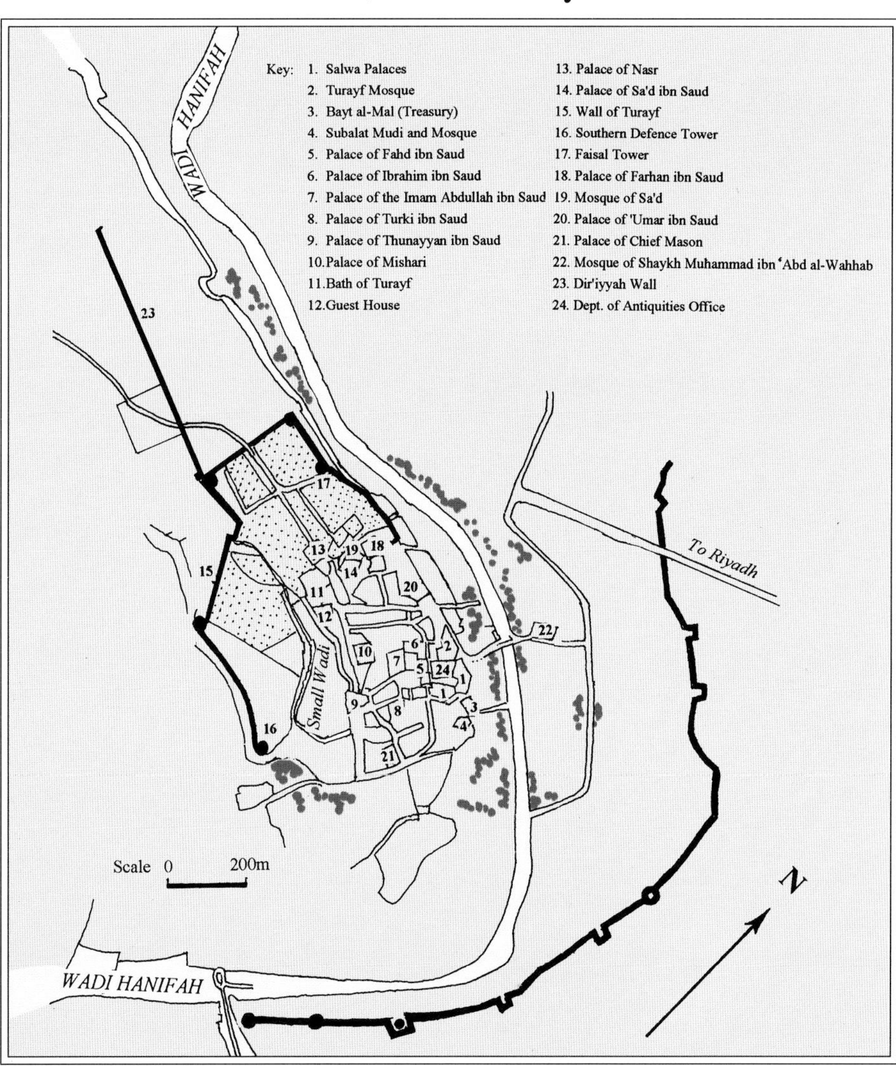

The Salwa Palaces

The palaces of the House of Saud bear the names of their final occupants. The Salwa Palaces complex, partly surrounded by a separate wall, formed the residence and seat of government of Saud the Great. His father the Imam 'Abd al-'Aziz also lived here, but Saud is said to have expanded the complex greatly to provide accommodation for his family. The complex included at least six palaces, including Saud's *majlis* or audience hall, a mosque and a well. Directly adjacent to it stood the Bayt al-Mal or Treasury. When Saud's son Abdullah became Imam in 1814, he left the palace complex to his mother and the rest of his father's immediate family.

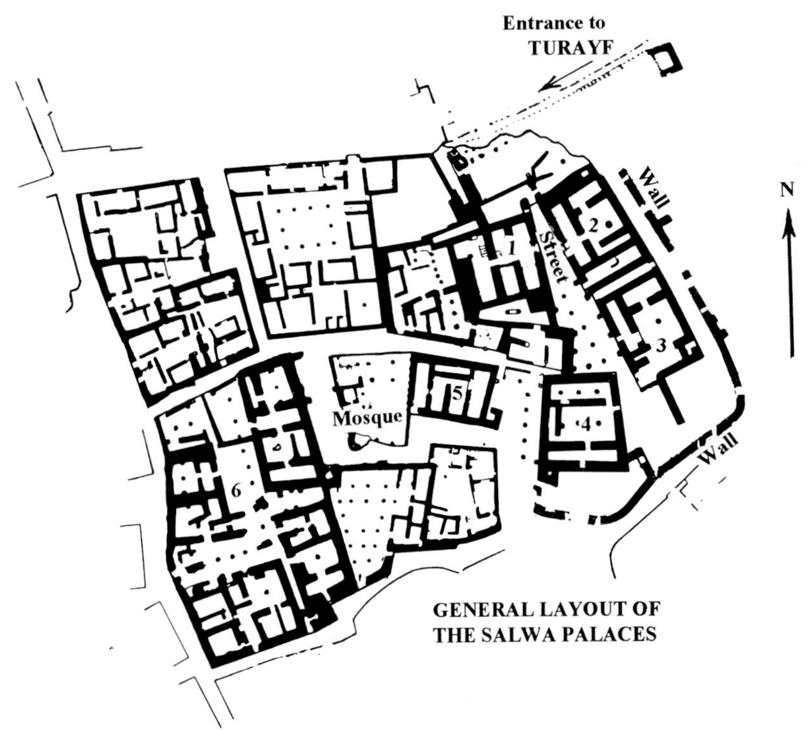

Above: The street between the Salwa Palaces is full of fallen stone column drums, perhaps remains of a raised walkway.

Right: The *majlis* of Saud the Great dominates the view of the Salwa Palaces from Wadi Hanifah. Remains of the wall which partly surrounded the palace complex, with a gateway through it, can be seen on the right.

Above: A typical long room at the rear of Salwa Palace no.1. These palaces were probably three-storey courtyard buildings. This palace was converted to storerooms by the Imam Abdullah in preparation for the siege.

Above left: A narrow street, sufficient for a camel and rider, passes between two of the Salwa Palaces to the gateway through the wall beyond.

Above: Tumbled tamarisk beams in Salwa Palace no.2 show how the floors were constructed.

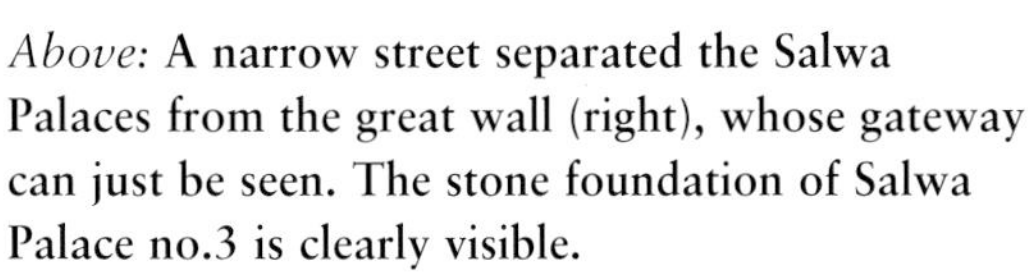

Above: A narrow street separated the Salwa Palaces from the great wall (right), whose gateway can just be seen. The stone foundation of Salwa Palace no.3 is clearly visible.

Right: This stone bowl, about 1m in diameter, can be seen in Salwa Palace no.2. It is almost the only old piece of equipment left in Turayf.

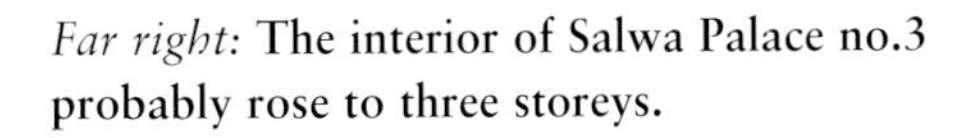

Far right: The interior of Salwa Palace no.3 probably rose to three storeys.

Left: The majlis or audience hall of Saud the Great (Salwa Palace no.4) was an imposing building which rose to four storeys. It is not thought to have been a courtyard building, at least at ground level. Here the Imam Saud received visitors and made himself accessible to his people, while judges settled disputes. There is evidence of a staircase on the south wall.

Below: The mosque of Saud the Great stands behind Salwa Palace no.5. Apart from fallen column drums, all that can now be seen is the *qiblah* wall and *mihrab* (right).

Right: Fallen column drums lie scattered on the floor of the *majlis* of Saud the Great.

Right: A view along the street between Salwa Palace no.5 (left) and the back of Saud the Great's *majlis* (right), towards the ruins of Salwa Palace no.1.

Below: Salwa Palace no.5 is in a relatively good state of preservation, with its long-drop privy rising to full height. Supports for the beams of the mosque of Saud the Great can be seen on the left-hand wall.

Right: Salwa Palace no.6 was a large, complex building. The fallen column drums outside it seem to have belonged to a covered – perhaps raised – walkway. This area is said to have been the ruling family's assembly court.

Below: Salwa Palace no.6 has an imposing tower by its entrance from the street.

Left: The inside of Salwa Palace no.6 has been much altered over time. This unusual early column is now embedded in a mud wall.

Below: A section of the wall of the Salwa Palaces adjacent to Salwa Palace no.6.

Turayf Mosque and Bayt al-Mal

The Turayf Mosque *(right)* as it is today is a different structure from the original, which was the principal mosque of Turayf. It was here that the Imam 'Abd al-'Aziz was assassinated in 1803 in revenge for Karbala. Ibn Bishr tells us that the assassin's knife was meant for Saud, who had led the assault on Karbala. On becoming Imam, Saud built a raised protected walkway from the Salwa Palaces to the mosque. Column drums and a finely built supporting wall for this can be seen below.

Right: The thick, curving wall of the Bayt al-Mal (Treasury) is all that remains of the original structure. Here the *zakah* and plunder from campaigns was gathered. Today the interior is full of ruined 20th century homes.

Subalat Mudi and the Palaces of Ibrahim and Fahd.

Right: The restored Mosque of Subalat Mudi has a semi-basement prayer hall beneath the main one above. In 1862, during his stay in Riyadh, Palgrave was told that the great mosque there also had a basement prayer hall.

Above: The Palace of Ibrahim is a well-preserved structure seen here against the skyline from near the Palace of Abdullah.

Above: The Subalah ("Legacy") of Mudi, the daughter of Shaykh Muhammad ibn 'Abd al-Wahhab, is the only structure in Turayf which preserves columns to a height of two storeys.

Top: A detail of the columns, lancets and ventilation triangles of the Subalat Mudi.

Below: The Palace of Fahd is preserved almost to its full height.

The Palaces of Abdullah and Turki

The Palace of the Imam Abdullah ibn Saud occupies a larger ground-plan than any of the Salwa Palaces with the possible exception of Salwa Palace no.6. The thickness of its walls at ground level suggests that it may have been no more than three storeys high, or perhaps even two, as described by Fathallah Sayigh. Fallen column drums bear witness to a once grand courtyard *(right)*. There were many rooms on both storeys *(bottom)*. Unusually, the palace may have had four long-drop privy towers.

Left: There was a large open space outside the Palace of Imam Abdullah. The present wall fronting the palace is 20th century and seems not to follow the original alignment.

Left: The great courtyard of the Palace of Imam Abdullah ibn Saud. The column bases are encircled by a kind of bench.

Below: Another unnamed early palace adjoins the Palace of Imam Abdullah.

Right: The Palace of Turki. The hole is said to have been made by one of Ibrahim Pasha's cannonballs. Ibn Bishr described the Turco-Egyptian bombardment in 1818 as "falling like rain".

Below: The Palace of Turki (left) looking towards the Palace of Imam Abdullah.

The Palace of Thunayyan and neighbouring palaces

The Palace of Thunayyan occupies an important defensive position commanding the small wadi which cuts into the south-eastern side of Turayf *(seen below)*. It was a large palace built out onto a solid revetment of finely masoned limestone. Shaykh Muhammad ibn 'Abd al-Wahhab is said to have resided here after his initial welcome by Muhammad ibn Saud, before moving to Bujayri on the other side of Wadi Hanifah. The palace's large courtyard *(right)* has an unusual triangular form. After the siege it was taken over by date-pressers, and their pressing bins for making date syrup can still be seen.

Opposite page: Two large unnamed palaces stand adjacent to the Palace of Thunayyan, commanding the wadi below.

The Palace of Mishari

Mishari ibn Saud ruled Dir'iyyah briefly after Ibrahim Pasha's departure, having ousted Muhammad ibn Mu'ammar. His large palace *(below)* was perhaps three-storeyed, and backs onto an area of early buildings like the unnamed palace seen against the skyline *(right)*.

Above: Decorative lancet and triangle detail, and long-drop privy tower, Palace of Mishari.

The Bath House

Turayf's bath house *(right)* was almost certainly a late addition to the site, built either by the Imam Saud or the Imam Abdullah. It had a hot room heated by a triple-arched brick furnace *(seen bottom right)*, a cold room *(centre right)* and changing room with benches and niches. Some of the arches and mud wall decoration *(below)* were unusual. Attached to the bath house was a guest house with a columned courtyard for important visitors. Department of Antiquities excavations revealed that the hot room was domed. Water was brought up by donkey from a well in the small wadi below. There were outlet pipes for disposing of waste water *(seen in the external wall, right)*.
A visualised reconstruction of the bath house is reproduced on pages 52-53.

The Palace of Nasr

The Palace of Nasr *(below)* was the first building in Turayf to be restored by the Department of Antiquities. Unusually, it is a single-storey building surrounding a large courtyard *(right)*.

Right: One of Turayf's main streets, running from the western gate to the centre of the town, passed between the Palace of Nasr *(right)* and the Palace of Sa'd *(left)*.

The Palace of Sa'd

The Palace of Sa'd, rebuilt during the 1980s, is the Department of Antiquities' most ambitious reconstruction effort – the best place to go to appreciate the imposing effect of Turayf's original palaces.

Above: The south-western corner of the Palace of Sa'd seen across the brickyard used during the restoration project.

Above right: The south-western corner of the palace consisted of a service courtyard used for animals, cooking and other household tasks.

Above: This aerial view of the Palace of Sa'd shows its courtyard form. It is built on three storeys, a height determined by the survival of the long-drop privy tower on the corner of the main block nearest to the camera.

Below: The restored Palace of Sa'd presents a striking contrast to the tumbled stone ruins in the western part of Turayf.

The Mosque of Sa'd and the Palace of Farhan

The Mosque of Sa'd *(below)* abuts the northern side of the Palace of Sa'd. The ***qiblah*** wall and ***mihrab*** *(bottom)* have been restored.

The ruined Palace of Farhan *(below)* lies just to the north of the Palace of Sa'd.

The Palace of 'Umar

The Palace of 'Umar is one of the most stylish and best-preserved palaces in Turayf. It has not been restored, but stands almost to its full height over-looking Wadi Hanifah. From Turayf itself it is not so imposing *(below)*.

Right: The Palace of 'Umar rose to at least three storeys.

Left: The Palace of 'Umar commands Wadi Hanifah and was built for defence on a revetment of cut limestone blocks, like the Palace of Thunayyan.

The Faisal Tower

The Faisal Tower *(right)* named after the Imam Abdullah's dashing brother, was built for artillery and commands a good view of Wadi Hanifah. It also commands the so-called "Mule Trail", one of the main access routes to Turayf.

Right: The "Mule Trail" leads up to the Faisal Tower from Wadi Hanifah, past a large unnamed palace on the left. The "Mule Trail" gave access to the great square of Turayf.

Below: The Faisal Tower contrasts with the eroded walls of western Turayf.

Below: The Faisal Tower was carefully restored by the Department of Antiquities in the late 1980s.

Western and eastern Turayf

The whole western end of Turayf *(below and bottom)* west of the Palaces of Nasr and Sa'd lies in ruins, partly because this area was never built up during the 20th century occupation of the site. The lower income groups seem to have lived here, although some of the surviving buildings on its eastern side are quite spacious. The walls were almost entirely of rough stone, sometimes laid in a herringbone pattern. They were then plastered in mud and so would have looked like mud brick buildings.

Right: An unnamed early palace on the eastern edge of Turayf, north of the chief mason's house.

Fortifications

Right: The corner watchtower on the southern Turayf wall.

Left: A corner tower near the house of the chief mason on the south-eastern edge of Turayf.

Left: Massive buttressed fortifications above Bulayda

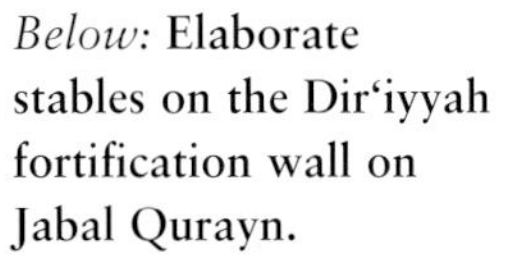

Below: Elaborate stables on the Dir'iyyah fortification wall on Jabal Qurayn.

Bibliography

Abbreviations

EI[1] *The Encyclopaedia of Islam* first edition, Leiden and London 1913-38.

EI[2] *The Encyclopaedia of Islam* second edition, Leiden and London 1960-86, in progress.

El-Abbasi, Aly Bey. *Travels of Ali Bey in Morocco, Tripoli, Cyprus, Egypt, Arabia, Syria and Turkey between the Years 1803 and 1807*. London, 1816.

Abu Hakima, A. *History of Eastern Arabia, 1750-1800 – the Rise and Development of Bahrain and Kuwait*. London, 1965. *The Modern History of Kuwait, 1750-1965*. London, 1983.

Anon. *Lam' al-Shihab*.

El-Ashiry, Hassan. "The rehabilitation of Ad-Dar'iyya ", *Art and Archaeology Research Papers*, pp.81-83. London, 1980.

Assah, A. *Miracle of the Desert Kingdom*. London, 1969.

Babeair, 'Abd al-Wahhab Salih. *Ottoman Penetration of the Eastern Region of the Arabian Peninsula, 1814-1841*. Ph.D thesis, University of Indiana. Ann Arbor, Michigan, 1985.

Bankes, W.J. *Narrative of the Life and Adventures of Giovanni Finati ... Who Made the Campaigns against the Wahabees*. 2 vols. London, 1830.

Benoist-Mechin. *Arabian Destiny*. London, 1957.

Brydges, Harford jones. *An Account of His Majesty's Mission to the Court of Persia in the Years 1807-11. To which is Appended a Brief History of the Wahauby*. 2 vols., London, 1834.

Burckhardt, J.L. *Travels in Arabia*. London, 1829. *Notes on the Bedouins and Wahabys*. London, 1830.

Chelhod, J. *Le désert et la gloire. Les mémoires d'un agent syrien de Napoléon, par Fathallah Sayigh*. Paris, 1991.

Corancez, L.A.O. de. *Histoire des Wahabis depuis leur origine jusqu'à la fin de 1809*. Paris, 1810.

Crabitès, Pierre. *Ibrahim of Egypt*. London, 1935.

Crichton, A. *History of Arabia, Ancient and Modern*. New York,1839.

Dari ibn Rashid. *Nubdhah Ta'rikhiyyah 'an Najd*. Riyadh, 1966.

De Gaury, G. *Rulers of Mecca*. London, 1951.

Department of Antiquities and Museums. *The Walls and Towers of Al-Turaif, Dir'iyah*. Riyadh, 1983. *The Turkish Bath and its Annexes, al-Turaif Quarter, al-Diriyah*. Riyadh, n.d.

Dickson, H.R.P. *The Arab of the Desert*. London, 1949. *Kuwait and her Neighbours*. London, 1956

Dickson, Violet. *Forty Years in Kuwait*. London, 1956.

Didier, Charles. *Séjour chez le Grand-Chérif de la Mekke*. Paris, 1857. Published in English as *Sojourn with the Grand Sharif of Makkah*, Cambridge 1985.

Dodwell, Henry. *The Founder of Modern Egypt*. Cambridge, 1931.

Dowson, V.H.W. "The Date and the Arab", *Journal of the Royal Central Asian Society* 36, pp.34-41, 1949.

Driault, E. *La formation de l'empire de Mohamed Aly de l'Arabie au Soudain 1814-1823*. Cairo, 1927.

Facey, W.H.D. *Riyadh – The Old City*. London, 1992. *The Story of the Eastern Province of Saudi Arabia*. London, 1994.

Freeman- Grenville, G.S.P. *The Muslim and Christian Calendars*. London, 1977

Gouldrup, L. "The Ikhwan Movement of Central Arabia", *Arabian Studies VI*, pp.161-169, 1982.

Great Britain, 1946 Naval Intelligence Division. *Western Arabia and the Red Sea*. Geographical Handbook Series B.R. 527. London, 1946.

Haarmann, U. "Murtada b. 'Ali b. 'Alawan's Journey Through Arabia in 1121/1709", in *Sources for the History of Arabia*, pp.247-251. Riyadh, 1979.

Habib, J.S. *Ibn Sa'ud's Warriors of Islam: the Ikhwan of Najd and their Role in the Creation of the Sa'udi Kingdom 1910-1930*. Leiden, 1978.

Hajji Khalfa. See Norberg.

Hitti, P.K. *History of the Arabs*. London, 1970.

Hogarth, D.G. *The Penetration of Arabia*. London, 1904.

Holden, D. and R. Johns. *The House of Saud*. London, 1982.

Ibn Battutah. *Voyages d'Ibn Batoutah*, vol.2. Arabic text with translation into French by C. Defrémery and B. Sanguinetti. Paris, 1854. *The Travels of Ibn Battuta A.D. 1325-1354*, vol.2. Translated, edited and annotated, from the text of Defrémery and Sanguinetti, by H.A.R. Gibb. Hakluyt Society, Cambridge, 1958.

Ibn Bishr, 'Uthman. *'Unwan al-Majd fi Ta'rikh Najd*. Maktabah al-Riyadh al-Hadithah, Riyadh, undated.

Ibn Ghannam, Husain. *Rawdat al-'Afkar wa'l-'Afham li-Murtad Hal al-'Imam wa-Ta'dad Ghazawat dhawi al-Islam*. Riyadh, 1381 AH.

Ibn 'Isa, Ibrahim *Ta'rikh ba'd al-Hawadith al-Waqa'a fi Najd*. Riyadh, undated.

Ibn Khaldun *The Muqaddimah. An Introduction to History*. Translated with an Introduction by Franz Rosenthal. 3 vols., Princeton, 1967.

Ibn Khamis, Abdullah. *Dir'iyyah*. Riyadh.

India Office Library and Records. G/29 Series – Factory Records Persia and the Persian Gulf. [On Grane/Kuwait]

Al-Jasir, Hamad. *Madinat al-Riyad 'abr Atwar al-Ta'rikh*. Riyadh, 1386 AH.

Jomard, E.F. *Notice géographique sur le pays de Nejd en Arabie centrale*. Paris,1823 [The same as "Notice géographique sur la carte du pays de Nedjd ..." in Mengin 1823]. *Etudes géographiques et historiques sur l'Arabie avec des observations sur l'état des affaires en Arabie ... Accompagnées d'une carte de l'Acyr et d'une carte générale de l'Arabie*; ... Paris, 1839.

Al-Juhany, U.M. *The History of Najd Prior to the Wahhabis: a Study of Social, Political and Religious Conditions in Najd During Three Centuries Preceding the Wahhabi Reform Movement*.Ph.D. thesis, University of Washington, published by University Microfilms, Ann Arbor, Michigan, 1983.

Kelly, J.B. *Britain and the Persian Gulf*. Oxford, 1968.

King, G. "Traditional Architecture in Najd, Saudi Arabia", *Proceedings of the Seminar for Arabian Studies 7*, pp.90-100, 1977. "Traditional Najdi Mosques", *Bulletin of the School of Oriental and African Studies* XLI pp.464-498, 1978. "Some European Travellers in Najd in the 19th and Early 20th Centuries", in *Sources for the History of Arabia* Part 2, p.255-265. Riyadh, 1979. "Some Examples of the Secular Architecture of Najd", *Arabian Studies* VI, pp.113-142, 1982. *The Historical Mosques of Saudi Arabia*. London, 1986. *The Islamic Building Tradition in Saudi Arabia*. Unpublished MS, undated.

Lacey, R. *The Kingdom*. London, 1981.

Lorimer, J.G. *Gazetteer of the Persian Gulf, 'Oman and Central Arabia,* 2 vols. Calcutta, 1908-15.

Mandaville, J.E. "The Ottoman Province of al-Hasa in the Sixteenth and Seventeenth Centuries", *Journal of the American Oriental Society 90*, pp.486-513, 1970. *The History of al-Hasa and its Fortresses and Fortifications*. SECON/ Building Conservation Technology Inc. Riyadh, 1983.

Margoliouth, D. "Wahhabiyya", *EI*[1] vol.4 part 2, pp.1086-1090, 1934.

McLoughlin, L.J. *Ibn Saud, Founder of a Kingdom*. London, 1993.

Mengin, F. *Histoire de l 'Egypte sous le gouvernement de Mohammed-Aly*, 2 vols.. Paris, 1823. *Histoire sommaire de l'Egypte sous le gouvernement de Mohammed-Aly ou récit des principaux événements qui ont eu lieu de l'an 1823 à l'an 1838. Précédé d'une introduction et service d'études géographiques et historiques sur l'Arabie par M. Jomard* ... [= Jomard 1839]. Paris, 1839

Monroe, E. Philby of Arabia. London, 1973.

Mousalli, M., F. Shaker and O.Mandily. *An Introduction to Urban Patterns in Saudi Arabia: the Central Region*. London, 1977.

Musil, Alois. *Northern Negd*. New York, 1928.

Niebuhr, C. *Description de l'Arabie*. Amsterdam, 1774

Norberg, C. *Gihan Numa* of Hajji Khalfah, tr. into Latin and ed. Norberg. Gotha, 1818. (Reprinted 1973).

O'Kinealy, J. "Translation of an Arabic Pamphlet on the History and Doctrines of the Wahhabis, Written by 'Abdullah, grandson of 'Abdul Wahhab, the Founder of Wahhabism", *Journal of the Bengal Asiatic Society* no.43, part 1, pp.68-82, 1874.

Palgrave, W.G. *Narrative of a Year's Journey Through Central and Eastern Arabia (1862-3)*. 2 vols., London, 1865.

Pelly, L. *Report on a Journey to Riyadh in Central Arabia, 1865*. Bombay, 1866. (Reprinted Cambridge 1978).

Philby, H. St.J. *The Heart of Arabia*. 2 vols., London, 1922. *Arabia of the Wahhabis*. London, 1928. "A Survey of Wahhabi Arabia, 1929", *Journal of the Royal Central Asian Society,* 16:4 (1929), pp.468-81, 1929. *Arabia*. London, 1930. *Sa'udi Arabia*. London, 1955. *Najd Diaries*. Unpublished manuscript diaries vols.1-4 in Middle East Centre, St. Antony's College, Oxford, n.d.

Pirenne, J. *À la découverte de l'Arabie*. Paris, 1958.

Al-Rashid, Madawi. *Politics in an Arabian Oasis. The Rashidi Tribal Dynasty*. London, 1991.

Al-Rashid, Z.M. *Su'udi Relations with Eastern Arabia and 'Uman (1800-1871)*. London, 1981.

Raunkiaer, B. *Through Wahhabiland on Camelback*. 1912. Introduced by G. de Gaury. London, 1969.

Rentz, G. *Muhammad ibn 'Abd al-Wahhab (1703/4-1792) and the Beginnings of Unitarian Empire in Arabia*. Ph.D thesis, Berkeley, California, 1947. "Al-Dir'iyya", *EI*[2] vol.2 pp.320-322, 1965. "Wahhabism and Saudi Arabia", in *The Arabian Peninsula – Society and Politics*, ed. Hopwood, pp.54-66. London, 1972. "Khadir, Banu", *EI*[2] vol.4, pp.905-906, 1978. "Philby as a Historian of Saudi Arabia", *Sources for the History of Arabia*, Part 2, pp.25-35. Riyadh, 1979.

Rihani, A. *Ibn Sa'oud of Arabia. His People and his Land*. London, 1928.

Rosenfeld, H. "The Social Composition of the Military in the Process of State Formation in the Arabian Desert", *Journal of the Royal Anthropological Institute* vol.95. In two parts, pp.75-86, 174-194, 1965.

Ross, E.C. *Memoir on Nejd*. Persian Gulf Administration Report, Govt. of India, 1879-80.

Rottiers, Le. *Itinéraire de Tiflis à Constantinople*. Brussels, 1829.

Sabini, J. *Armies in the Sand. The Struggle for Mecca and Medina*. London, 1981.

SADLEIR, G.F. "Account of a Journey from Katif on the Persian Gulf to Yamboo on the Red Sea...", *Transactions of the Literary Society of Bombay* III, pp.449-493, 1823. *Diary of a Journey across Arabia (1819)*. Bombay, 1866. (Reprinted with an Introduction by F.M. Edwards, Cambridge 1977).

SALDANA, J.A. *Précis of Nejd Affairs, 1804-1904*. Simla, 1904.

SAYIGH, FATHALLAH *Le désert et la gloire. Les Mémoires d'un agent syrien de Napoléon*. Translated, edited and introduced by Joseph Chelhod, Paris, 1991.

SEETZEN, U. Letters to Baron von Zach in *Monatliche Correspondenz* vol.12. Gotha, 1805. (No. XXII of Sept. 1805, pp.234-241, on Reinaud.)

SECON (SAUDI ENGINEERING CONSULTANTS BUREAU) *The History of al-Hasa and its Forts and Fortifications*. Riyadh, Dept. of Antiquities and Museums, 1983.

EL-SHAAFY, M. "The Military Organisation of the First Sa'udi State", *The Annual of Leeds University Oriental Society* vol.VII, 1969-1973. Leiden, 1975.

SHAMEKH, A. *Spatial Patterns of Bedouin Settlement in al-Qasim Region, Saudi Arabia*. Lexington, Kentucky, 1975.

AL-SHIHABI, M. "Filaha", *EI²* vol.2 pp.899-901, 1965.

STEVENS, J.H. "Oasis Agriculture in the Central and Eastern Arabian Peninsula", *Geography* 57, pp.321-326, 1972.

AL-SUWAIDA, A. *Najd fi'l-Ams al-Qarib*. Riyadh, 1983.

TRENCH, R. *Arabian Travellers*. London, 1986.

TROELLER, G. *The Birth of Saudi Arabia*. London, 1976.

TUSON, P. *The Records of the British Residency and Agencies in the Persian Gulf*. India Office Library and Records, London, 1979.

VALENTIA, GEORGE VISCOUNT. *Voyages and Travels to India, Ceylon, the Red Sea, Abyssinia and Egypt*. London, 1809.

WARDEN, F., S. HENNELL, A. KEMBALL AND H. DISBROWE. "Historical Sketch of the Wahabee Tribe of Arabs, from the year 1795 ... to the year 1853", in *Selections from the Records of the Bombay Government*, New Series, no.XXIV, 1856, pp.428-460 Bombay, 1856. [Re-printed Cambridge 1985.]

WEYGAND, LE. GÉNÉRAL. *Histoire militaire de Mohammed Aly et ses fils*. 2 vols., Paris, 1936.

WILBERDING, S. *Guidebook to the Ruins in Dir'aiyah*. Riyadh, 1987.

WINDER, R. BAYLY. *Saudi Arabia in the Nineteenth Century*. London, 1965.

AL-YASSINI, A. *Religion and State in the Kingdom of Saudi Arabia*. Boulder, Colorado, 1985.

ZIRIKLY, KHAIR AL-DIN. *Shibh al-Jazirah fi Ahd al-Malik 'Abd al-'Aziz*, 4 vols., Beirut, 1970.

THE RULERS OF THE HOUSE OF SAUD

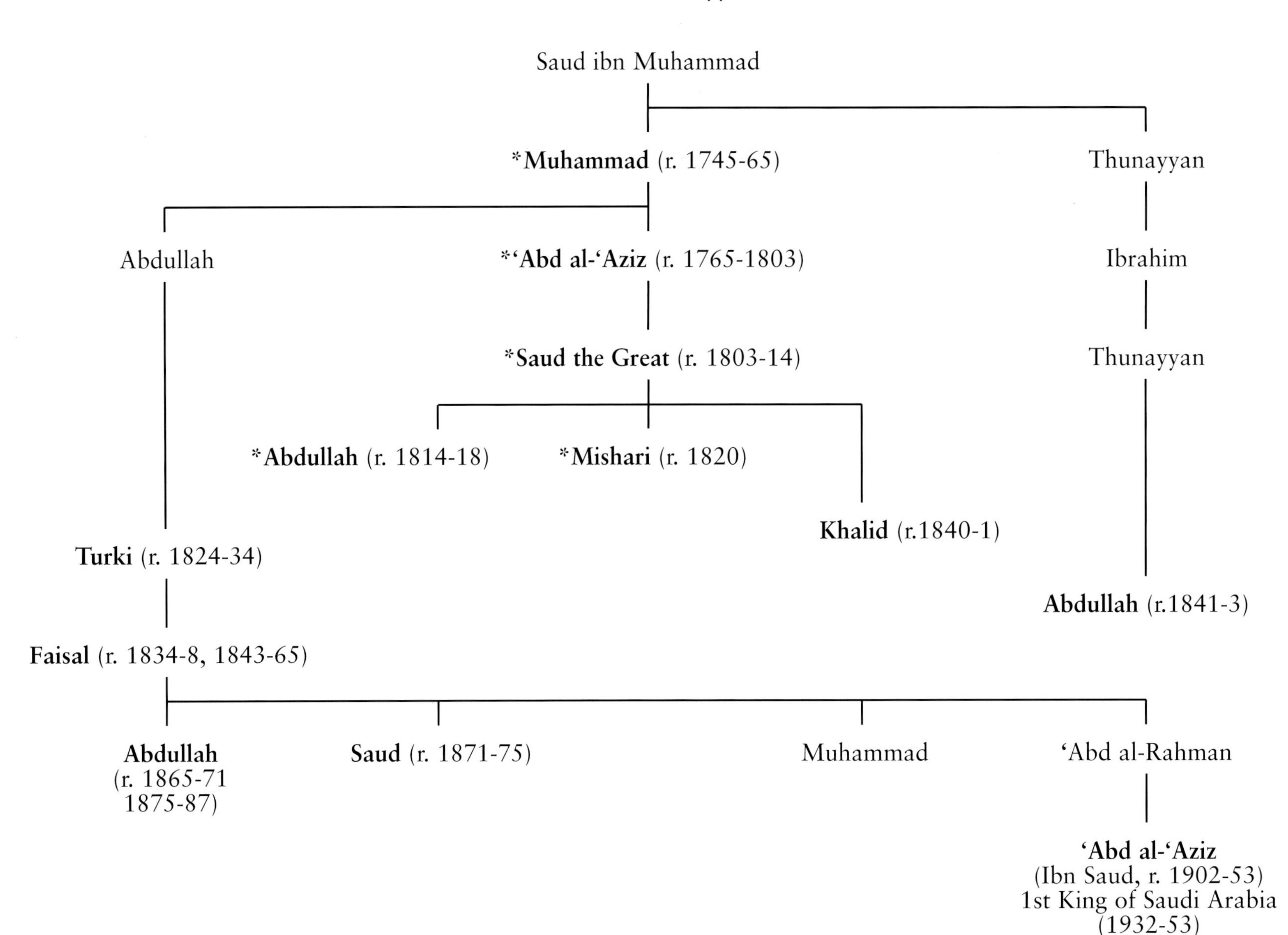

Index